KU-282-793

Contents

WRITER-FILES

General Editor: Simon Trussler

Associate Editor: Malcolm Page

File on
FRAYN

Compiled by Malcolm Page

Methuen Drama

A Methuen Drama Book

First published in Great Britain 1994
by Methuen Drama,
an imprint of Reed Consumer Books Ltd.,
Michelin House, 81 Fulham Road, London SW3 6RB,
and Auckland, Melbourne, Singapore, and Toronto,
and distributed in the United States of America by
Heinemann, a division of Reed Publishing (USA) Inc.,
361 Hanover Street, Portsmouth, New Hampshire 03801-3959

Copyright in the compilation
©1994 by Malcolm Page
Copyright in the series format
©1994 by Methuen Drama
Copyright in the editorial presentation
©1994 by Simon Trussler

ISBN 0 413 65310 2

A CIP catalogue record for this book
is available at the British Library

Typeset in 9/10 Times by
L. Anderson Typesetting,
Woodchurch, Kent TN26 3TB

Printed in Great Britain
by Cox and Wyman Ltd.,
Cardiff Road, Reading

Front cover photograph of
Michael Frayn by Jillian Edelstein

The theatre is, by its nature, an ephemeral art: yet it is a daunting task to track down the newspaper reviews, or contemporary statements from the writer or his director, which are often all that remain to help us recreate some sense of what a particular production was like. This series is therefore intended to make readily available a selection of the comments that the critics made about the plays of leading modern dramatists at the time of their production — and to trace, too, the course of each writer's own views about his work and his world.

In addition to combining a uniquely convenient source of such elusive *documentation*, the 'Writer-Files' series also assembles the *information* necessary for readers to pursue further their interest in a particular writer or work. Variations in quantity between one writer's output and another's, differences in temperament which make some readier than others to talk about their work, and the variety of critical response, all mean that the presentation and balance of material shifts between one volume and another: but we have tried to arrive at a format for the series which will nevertheless enable users of one volume readily to find their way around any other.

Section 1, 'A Brief Chronology', provides a quick conspective overview of each playwright's life and career. *Section 2* deals with the plays themselves, arranged chronologically in the order of their composition: information on first performances, major revivals, and publication is followed by a brief synopsis (for quick reference set in slightly larger, italic type), then by a representative selection of the critical response, and of the dramatist's own comments on the play and its theme.

Section 3 offers concise guidance to each writer's work in non-dramatic forms, while *Section 4*, 'The Writer on His Work', brings together comments from the playwright himself on more general matters of construction, opinion, and artistic development. Finally, *Section 5* provides a bibliographical guide to other primary and secondary sources of further reading, among which full details will be found of works cited elsewhere under short titles, and of collected editions of the plays — but not of individual titles, particulars of which will be found with the other factual data in Section 2.

The 'Writer-Files' hope by striking this kind of balance between information and a wide range of opinion to offer 'companions' to the study of major playwrights in the modern repertoire — not in that dangerous pre-digested fashion which can too readily quench the desire to read the plays themselves, nor so prescriptively as to allow any single line of approach to predominate, but rather to encourage readers to form their own judgements of the plays in a wide-ranging context.

Michael Frayn, suggests the critic Michael Billington on page 28 of this collection, has 'the rare ability to construct farcical comedy around philosophical principles'. The philosopher whose principles seem most to have attracted Frayn is, of course, Wittgenstein — whose many changes of mind and approach certainly accorded with one of his few constant beliefs, that 'philosophy is not a theory but an activity'. Since it is an activity which more than most indulges, as he declared, in 'language games', the fit is excellent — between the active language game which is philosophy, and the game-playing mesh of language and action which is drama.

Frayn himself adds Freud to the mix, in reckoning that *Noises Off* was 'more a Freudian play than a Wittgensteinian' (page 31). For good measure, we might also, with a due pinch of salt, stir in Bergson's view of laughter as a response to the mechanistic — that automatic piloting or meta-behaviour into which we all absurdly slip in moments of tragical or farcical crisis. Such a complex support system of theory would overwhelm most writers, confronted with the no less complex demands of entertaining an audience: yet how much more clearly than (say) Stoppard does Frayn reveal to us that the foolishnesses and foibles of his characters do merit our observation — sometimes even our sympathy — as well as our laughter; and how much more than (say) Ayckbourn does he persuade us that the mechanics of farcical plotting can be as much matters of human predilection as of dramatic construction.

I can remember now, as one of those rare occasions when laughter drifts from the delighted into the helpless and towards the almost painful, my first reading, during Frayn's early career as a humorous columnist, of those parodic pocket 'autobiographies' of Mozart and T. S. Eliot, written after the manner of their subjects. The element of pastiche was postmodern well before its time: more to the point, and detached from critical jargon, it remains immensely funny — yet also, as when watching the umpteenth TV rerun of *Clockwise*, there is the enduring pleasure of observing technique consummately translated into activity, long after the inevitable fading of the first 'sudden glory'.

On page 77, Frayn suggests that all his plays may be about 'the way in which we impose our ideas upon the world around us'. In the crushing of his characters between the hapless solipsism of their endeavours and the resolute infrangibility of the actual lies a good deal not only of the humour of his plays but of the shock of recognition they deliver.

Simon Trussler

1933 8 September, born in Mill Hill, London. 'My father was a rep. for an asbestos company and very keen that I should follow him into the business. . . . My mother died when I was a boy. She had worked in shops, in Harrods. I discovered recently that she had also modelled for Harrods' (interviewed by Craig Raine, *Quarto*, March 1980, p. 3).

1935 Family moved to Ewell, to the south west of London. 'Everyone puts down the suburbs, but they're very pleasant places to live. It's quite amazing how little they've changed in forty years. They should be taken more seriously.' Attended 'a dreadful private day school at Sutton' — 'an imposing brick facade disguising an awful lot of corrugated iron', where 'the headmaster used to cane about twenty boys every morning after prayers'.

1945 To Kingston Grammar School — 'merely rather dull and shabby'.

1952-54 National Service in Royal Artillery. After basic training, sent to Cambridge for a year to learn Russian.

1954-57 Attended Emmanuel College, Cambridge, on State Scholarship. Read Russian and French in his first year, but found that, though 'he got on well with the language, when it came to the literature he couldn't see for the life of him what to write down'. Changed to Moral Sciences (now Philosophy) for his second and third years. Wrote prolifically for *Varsity* and *Granta*, and in 1957 wrote *Zounds!*, the annual Footlights' show. 'I enjoyed [Cambridge] immensely. Shamefully, because I'm very conscious of what an awful thing it is to say, I liked the sheer exclusiveness of the place, the feeling of being somewhere difficult to get into, full of the sort of people I'd never met before, people with a certain style, a certain sense of irony, understatement, self-mockery, dash, and panache' (interviewed by Benedict Nightingale, *New York Times Magazine*, 8 December 1985, p. 127). 'The art-forms most passionately aspired to were musical comedy, revue, jazz, singing to a guitar, posters — anything that was predominantly entertaining and stylish. Our brand of humour was what was then called by its admirers "off-beat", which meant whimsical; carefully artless sub-Thurber cartoons' (Frayn, *World Authors 1950-70*, p. 493).

1957-59 Reporter for the *Manchester Guardian*, based in

Manchester. Covered Harold Macmillan's visit to Moscow in 1959. 'The *Guardian* system seemed to me ideal. They didn't give you any formal training; you did whatever came up, a lot of routine reporting but also a lot of colour writing, interviews with the last surviving clog-maker, that kind of thing. You were also expected to do a lot of reviewing, local theatres, films, book reviews, and I wrote a fair number of leaders, often humorous ones of incredible leaden portentous facetiousness. . . . It was a marvellous life, which would probably be impossible for anyone starting in journalism now, because of union rules. I very much took to newspapers' (interviewed by Miriam Gross, *Sunday Telegraph*, 30 November 1986, p. 17).

1959-62 Based in London, wrote 'Miscellany' column for *Manchester Guardian* three times a week.

1960 Married Gillian Palmer. They had three daughters, and lived in Blackheath, London.

1962-68 Wrote a weekly humorous column for *The Observer*. Published *The Day of the Dog*, a collection of *Guardian* columns, 1962.

1963 Published *The Book of Fub*, more collected *Guardian* columns. Edited *The Best of Beachcomber* (Heinemann).

1964 Published *On the Outskirts*, collected *Observer* columns. Edited, with Bamber Gascoigne, *Timothy*, a tribute to Timothy Birdsall, Cambridge cartoonist who had died young.

1965 Publication of his first novel, *The Tin Men*.

1966 Second novel, *The Russian Interpreter*, wins Maugham Award

1967 Third novel, *Towards the End of Morning*, wins Hawthornden Award. *At Bay in Gear Street*, collected *Observer* columns, published.

1968 The novel *A Very Private Life* published. First television play, *Jamie on a Flying Visit*.

1969 *Birthday* televised.

1970 His first stage play, *The Two of Us*, staged at the Garrick Theatre, London.

1971 *The Sandboy* staged at Greenwich Theatre.

1972 Wrote comedy series for BBC TV, *Beyond a Joke*.

1973 Publication of his novel *Sweet Dreams*. *Laurence Sterne Lived Here* televised by BBC TV.

1974 His philosophical work, *Constructions*, published.

1975 *Alphabetical Order* staged at Hampstead Theatre. Wrote *Making Faces*, a comedy series for Eleanor Bron on BBC TV, and *Imagine a City Called Berlin* for BBC TV (later presented TV programmes on Vienna, travelling by train across Australia, and Jerusalem).

1976 *Donkeys' Years* staged at Globe Theatre, London, and *Clouds* at Hampstead Theatre.

1978 *Balmoral* staged at Guildford (also known as *Liberty Hall*). His translation of Chekhov's *The Cherry Orchard* staged at the National Theatre.

1979 His translation of Tolstoi's *The Fruits of Enlightenment* staged at the National Theatre.

1980 *Make and Break* staged at Lyric Theatre, Hammersmith.

1981 Separated. Subsequently living with Claire Tomalin, biographer, in Camden Town, north London.

1982 *Noises Off* staged at Lyric Theatre, Hammersmith, then transferring for a long West End run at the Savoy Theatre.

1984 *Benefactors* staged at Vaudeville Theatre, *Wild Honey*, his adaptation of Chekhov's play without a title, at the National Theatre, and his translation of Anouilh's *Number One* at the Queen's Theatre.

1985 Translation of Chekhov's *Three Sisters* staged in Manchester, and in London in 1987.

1986 His first film script, *Clockwise*. Translation of Chekhov's *The Seagull* staged at Watford, and later by the RSC at the Swan Theatre, Stratford-upon-Avon, and the Barbican in London. Adaptation of Yuri Trifonov's *Exchange* for BBC radio, later staged in Southampton, 1989, and in London, 1990.

1988 Translation of Chekhov's *Uncle Vanya* staged at Vaudeville

Theatre. *The Sneeze*, his version of four short plays and four short stories by Chekhov, staged at Aldwych Theatre.

1989 Divorced. *The Trick of It*, his sixth novel, the first for sixteen years. Television film, *First and Last*.

1990 *Look Look* staged at Aldwych Theatre.

1991 Seventh novel, *A Landing on the Sun*, published. Won the *Sunday Express* 'Book of the Year' award.

1992 Eighth novel, *Now You Know*, published, and film of *Noises Off* released.

1993 29 July, *Here* staged at Donmar Warehouse, directed by Michael Blakemore. Married Claire Tomalin.

1994 Adapted his novel, *A Landing on the Sun*, for BBC TV. *Jamie on a Flying Visit* being extended for possible production by Scottish TV, and the novel, *Towards the End of Morning*, being 'developed' by Granada TV.

a: Stage Plays

The Two of Us

Four one-act plays, for performance by the same two actors.
First production: Garrick Th., London, 30 July 1970,
   preceded by tour to Cambridge, Brighton, and Southsea
   (dir. Mark Cullingham; with Richard Briers and
   Lynn Redgrave).
Published: Fontana, 1970; in *Listen to This* (Methuen, 1990),
   p. 25-118.

The first [Black and Silver], *is no more than a revue
sketch: a young husband and wife have a night
disturbed by their baby son, whom they have been so
foolish as to bring on holiday with them to their old
honeymoon hotel. Mr. Briers takes falls every time he is
roused from bed. Miss Redgrave feigns sleep. In the next
playlet* [The New Quixote] *she is seen as a bachelor
girl, getting on a bit, who has thoughtlessly allowed
a young stranger, met at a party, to come home with
her. Comic embarrassment and subterfuge when she
discovers that the young man, a mother's boy, addicted
to hi-fi and a remorseless system of self-questioning
which undermines his every conclusion, has decided to
move in on her permanently. The progress of the play,
which is charming, shows the girl, whose first reactions
are to get rid of the enthusiastic swain, slowly come
round to a mothering, not to say affectionate position
herself. She very subdued, he a lovely study of a
thoroughly mixed up autodidact who is clearly never
going to settle down. . . . After the interval, something
with a touch of the morbid* [Mr. Foot], *veering indeed
towards a kind of crazy pathos: here Miss Redgrave is a
suburban hysteric (to say the least) bored to a point of
being driven almost out of her mind by a morose
husband whose habit of wagging his foot as he sits
reading, whose snubs and grunts and scoldings, are*

somehow obliterating her identity. . . . I thought this was the best of the four. The last play [Chinamen], *which excited the audience's admiration for the high-spirited farcical twists and the ingenuity whereby a couple of players manage to people a bungalow with five people (two hosts and three visible guests) seemed to me rather protracted. But the trick of making one player exit and immediately enter as someone else on the far side of the stage never seems to pall.*

Philip Hope-Wallace, *The Guardian*, 31 July 1970

[*Black and Silver*] comes as close to the humour and intimacy of marital sex as any play I remember. Unfortunately it's the only one in which Frayn finds exactly the right length to contain his invention.

Ronald Bryden, *The Observer*, 2 Aug. 1970

What is disconcerting about [*Black and Silver* and *The New Quixote*] is not so much their thrift — material that would barely furnish forth a comic column being deemed, apparently, quite adequate for a one-act play — as their extreme banality. . . . [*Chinamen*] has the wit, brisk pace, and close observation conspicuously lacking elsewhere.

Hilary Spurling, *Plays and Players*, Sept. 1970, p. 36

[Frayn describes the whole experience — seeking a director, re-writing, the ups and downs of the pre-London tour — in 'On the Roller-Coaster', *The Observer*, 2 Aug. 1970.]

The Sandboy

First production: Greenwich Th., London, 16 Sept. 1971
(dir. Robert Chetwyn; with Joe Melia as Phil and Eleanor Bron as Rose).
Unpublished: script withdrawn.

The imposed shape is that of a television inquiry into a typical day in Phil Schaffer's life, spreading cables and artificiality all over the ginger fitted carpets. As he sees it, that should be a day of easy, modest meritocratic success; shots of him at his desk, against his crowded Hampstead bookshelves, poring over his perspex model of Rome redesigned as a fun city, hobnobbing with the best and nicest minds of his generation. Instead, the only friends to drop in are the lamentable Colin and Sheila, locked out of their house next door as a result of one of their endless quarrels. Colin and Sheila are all the things a rational man would like to edit out of his life — incompetence, mindless aggression, misfortune so chronic that they seem to seek it out with perverse relish. But the reason Phil would really like to bar them from his house and public image is his suspicion that they are the definition of his success. His sense of himself as a fortunate man depends on the majority's misfortune. His happiness is perpetually gnawed by fear and guilt; guilt at possessing it, at secretly hating anyone who symbolizes its precariousness.

Ronald Bryden, *The Observer*, 26 Sept. 1971

[*The Sandboy*] raises any number of fascinating issues: the elusive nature of happiness; the fraudulence of material success; the phoneyness of the Stringalong life-style; the creeping tyranny of sociological jargon; the power of the camera to turn us all into Uber-marionettes. But although Mr. Frayn has aired enough ideas to keep a newspaper columnist going for months and although he has created a totally credible hero, he has still not written a satisfactory play. . . . By giving us a solo portrait without any adequate surrounds (contrast, say *The Philanthropist*, where the minor characters have an organic life of their own) Frayn draws the sting from much of his satire. . . . While there is no shortage of ideas, there is a surprising lack of theatrical invention.

Michael Billington, *Plays and Players*, Nov. 1970, p. 47

It contained half a dozen excellent situations and scores of splendidly funny lines, every one of them pin-pricking some all too familiar aspect of contemporary life among (we may as well admit it) the brighter section of the community. It also enabled Joe Melia to give a brilliantly observed performance as the Sandboy: a successful young-middle-aged architect-planner who is also a contented husband and father — and somehow deeply ashamed of himself for being all these things. 'Some people have a sex problem', he cries, 'some people have a race problem — I have a smugness problem'. 'I was much happier', he tries to persuade himself, 'when I wasn't so happy'.

J. W. Lambert, 'Plays in Performance',
Drama, Winter 1971, p. 19

Alphabetical Order

Play in two acts.

First production: Hampstead Th., London, 11 Mar. 1975, transferred to
    Mayfair Th., 8 Apr. 1975 (dir. Michael Rudman; with Barbara Ferris
    as Leslie, Billie Whitelaw as Lucy, and Dinsdale Landen as John).
First American production: Long Wharf Th., New Haven, 8 Oct. 1976
    (dir. Steven Robman).
Published: with *Donkey's Years* (Eyre Methuen, 1977); in *Plays: One.*

*Alphabetical Order is set in the reference library of a somewhat
rundown provincial paper: as the play begins we find it inhabited
by a collection of crumbling desks, filing cabinets, and people —
among them Billie Whitelaw as the librarian/den mother, a lady
given to providing sustenance both sexual and otherwise for a
bunch of reporters who seem urgently in need of the kiss of life.
Chief among them is Dinsdale Landen, offering quite possibly the
comic performance of the year as a leader writer incapable of
starting a sentence without at least two double negatives and
a qualifying clause, the kind of man who comes through doors
murmuring 'on the other hand' and, in his own definition, a
perambulating heap of blancmange. Into the midst of this cosy,
decaying community erupts an assistant librarian (Barbara
Ferris, brisk) determined to bring order, sense, and logic with
her. She succeeds, though not before the paper has closed down,
presumably through lack of interest — as Landen says, the trouble
with it is that it's produced by the kind of people who read it.*

Sheridan Morley, *Shooting Stars* (London, 1983), p. 14-15

If you read it, you get the clear impression that it's a good part for Lucy
and that Leslie is very underwritten. In fact, I've seen several productions of it now and Leslie *always* wins on the stage. There's no way
of playing Lucy to make her more interesting than Leslie. Leslie's just a
much more interesting character. Partly because Lucy's over-written as a
part. She says too much about herself; she explains herself too much.
Leslie says very little, but there's a lot going on. Actresses absolutely get
their teeth into that part. It's not what I intended. I intended it to be fairly
evenly balanced and perhaps secretly I was being a bit over-sympathetic
towards Lucy, the untidy one. But as played, it's very difficult for any
actress doing Lucy to make her half as interesting as Leslie. It's very

curious how things come out on the stage. One's always learning appalling lessons about things not turning out as you expect. . . .

Most people argued that the end was dramatically terrible because it hadn't been prepared. In fact, of course, the characters do talk about the frightful state of the paper during Act I. But it was intended as a surprise.

> Frayn, interviewed by Craig Raine, 'The Quarto Interview',
> *Quarto*, No. 4 (Mar. 1980), p. 3, 4

I think *Alphabetical Order* is about the *interdependence* of order and disorder — about how any excess of the one makes you long for the other — about how the very possibility of the one implies the existence of the other.

> Frayn, 'Introduction', *Plays: One* (1985), p. xii

Only Bernard Gallagher was given a real, if minor character, in the person of a reporter who chattered spasmodically to disguise the fact that he was deaf, and infused into him a watchful humanity most welcome amid all these cardboard cut-outs.

> J. W. Lambert, 'Plays in Performance', *Drama*, Summer 1975, p. 41

The relationship between [Lucy and Leslie] is the best work in the play — it's good theatre. . . . Much of the rest, though, is too literary and schematic to work well dramatically. Some of the lines fall with as much inevitability as notes in a scale — you can hear members of the audience whispering their anticipation. This may indicate unerring craftsmanship; it also suggests a lack of flight. Arnold and John are a double act which makes sense on paper but is too pat on the stage. Arnold has reduced virtually all conversation to a shorthand of grunts leavened with wry one-liners of classical austerity. John declaims in Levinesque clusters of subordinate clauses and punctuates with conversational tics, particularly (and *ad nauseam*), 'as it were'.

> W. Stephen Gilbert, *Plays and Players*, May 1975, p. 22-3

Frayn is not a theatrical storyteller and when he attempts to gather up the threads of his action he comes near to choking himself with them. The play is most alive in its details, mostly affectionate, occasionally lethal: as when Leslie breaks open a first-aid box while everybody else is hunting for the key. That *is* an image; I would call it meaningful. Mr. Frayn's play survives its narrative deficiencies.

> Robert Cushman, 'From Frayn to Beckett',
> *The Observer*, 16 Mar. 1975

Donkeys' Years

Play in three acts.

First production: Globe Th., London, 15 July 1976 (dir. Michael
 Rudman; with Penelope Keith, later Anna Massey, as Lady Driver;
 Peter Barkworth, later Paul Eddington, as Headingley; Peter Jeffrey,
 later John Quayle, as Buckle; Andrew Robertson, later Ian Hogg, as
 Snell; Julian Curry, later John Quentin, as Quine; Harold Innocent,
 later Michael Rothwell, as Sainsbury; Jeffrey Wickham as Tate; and
 John Harding, later Christopher Northey, as Taylor).

First American production: New Th. of Brooklyn, 11 Mar. 1987
 (dir. Steve Stettler).

Television: ATV, Jan. 1980 (dir. Kenneth Ives; with Penelope Keith as
 Lady Driver, Colin Blakely as Headingly, Robert Lang as Buckle,
 Denholm Elliott as Quine, Timothy Bateson as Sainsbury, and
 Christopher Benjamin as Tate). Released by Precision Video, 1981.

Published: with *Alphabetical Order* (Eyre Methuen, 1977); in *Plays: One.*

In form the play is like a farcical English version of That
Championship Season. *The setting is the quad of a minor
Oxbridge college, the occasion a reunion dinner. And Frayn gets
some good laughs out of the middle-class embarrassment and
nervous male heartiness with which the guests greet each other
after twenty years. There is the junior government minister full
of armour-plated niceness, the caustic civil servant who is a
departmental Diogenes, the camp curate from Small Heath,
eternally roguish, the ghost-writer who hands out cards like a
Midlands car-salesman, and the back-slapping surgeon who
talks about removing people's waterworks. The two funniest
characters, however, are a karate-chopping Scottish scientist
who once seen is never remembered and the Master's wife, who
is now a lay judicial figure but who used to be an injudicious lay.
But having meticulously established a framework of social
comedy, Frayn then fills it with scrambling, door-banging farce.
The key joke is that the Master's wife, sniffing out an old lover,
finds herself nocturnally trapped among these roystering rowdies.*
Michael Billington, *The Guardian*, 16 July 1976

In *Donkeys' Years* middle-aged men find themselves confronted by the
perceptions they formed of each other — and of themselves — when

they were young, and by the styles of being they adopted then to give themselves shape in each other's eyes, and in their own. In the ensuing years they have all, consciously or unconsciously, slipped out of these shells, and when for one night they try to re-inhabit them the effect is as absurd as wearing outgrown clothes would be.

Frayn, 'Introduction', *Plays: One* (1985), p. xiii

Frayn manages to combine cool observation of a milieu and its characters with a kind of delight that they all exist, with their absurdities and eccentricities. His humour is rarely cruel, even when perhaps it should be, and in this play his dramatic technique, working up towards the complications of the last act, is remarkably assured.

John Elsom, *The Listener*, 22 July 1976, p. 90

These characters, reverting to type, can't sustain more than a bright comic anecdote. They are not representative of a generation other than having been at the same college. . . . [Frayn] can't, as David Hare achieved in *Teeth 'n' Smiles*, open up the play to make a real comment on English educational scars — or even hint at the need to evade Oxbridge's snobbish brand of shrapnel. 'See you again in twenty years', announces the Head Porter at the end, with genuine pride. It's a statement untarnished with the engaging comic unease of the first act. During the last act the characters behave exactly like their counterparts in a Brian Rix farce — what gives them superior status is merely the fact of having been to Oxbridge. Frayn's boldest stroke of comic invention is to have introduced Penelope Keith's Lady Driver into the all-male company.

Peter Ansorge, *Plays and Players*, Sept. 1976, p. 31

The pecking order is deftly established, with the MP and his consultant surgeon buddy at the top of the heap, subtly patronizing the others as they sit in dense cigar smog, flushed with the founders' port, considering the other paths their lives might have taken, and the priceless value of a university tradition that enables them to sit and talk about whether they ought to be sitting down and talking. All of which might still miss the point without the superb casting of Michael Rudman's production. *Donkeys' Years* is above all an actors' play, as its comedy resides so much in the gradations of English embarrassment and class feeling which we express far more through inflection and gesture than words. Peter Barkworth and Peter Jeffrey, for instance, have duologues circling around repetitions of the same phrase which means virtually nothing until accompanied by lunging handshakes and extravagant leg sweeps

17

which cover inactivity and mental blankness with a great show of superfluous activity.

Irving Wardle, The Times, 16 July 1976

See also:

J. R. Brown, *A Short Guide to Modern British Drama* (London, 1982), p. 61-3.

Clouds

Play in two acts.

First production: Hampstead Th., London, 16 Aug. 1976 (dir. Michael Rudman; with Nigel Hawthorne as Owen and Barbara Ferris as Mara).

Revived: Duke of York's Th., London, 1 Nov. 1978 (dir. Michael Rudman; with Tom Courtenay as Owen and Felicity Kendal as Mara).

First American production: New Arts Th., Dallas, 24 Oct. 1985 (dir. Stephen Hollis).

Published: Eyre Methuen, 1977; in *Plays: One*.

Clouds is set in Cuba — or at any rate an empty blue sky with beneath it just six chairs and a table. Into this void step Mara and Owen, two English writers come to report on life after the revolution. She is a lady novelist of the Edna O'Brien variety; he a jumpy, neurotic journalist — 'one always feels different about a country after lunch'. After some preliminary skirmishings, when each takes the other to be Cuban, it turns out that they are reporting for rival colour supplements. Accompanying them on the tour of the country is Angel, their slow-moving, slow-talking Cuban guide. 'I theenk we go now, I theenk it's time, I theenk. . . .' Angel spends much time pondering aloud on the patronizing nature of visitors coming to his country, and on man in general. Also on the sightseeing tour is Ed, an idealistic academic from the wilds of Illinois, who, on visiting a new town site, manages to see future socialist worlds in piles of industrial sand. Finally there is Hilberto, the party's happy-go-lucky, cigar-smoking driver. Is he the real Cuba? One after another, this male quartet turn hot and cold over Mara, whose allurements colour their views somewhat of the factories, sawmills, and collective farms they are taken to see. What noble minds, laid waste by English skirt!

Dave Robins, Plays and Players, Oct. 1976, p. 27

[*Clouds*] was originally written for television, but the BBC and all the commercial companies said they wouldn't be able to do it because it would need doing on film in somewhere like Spain. So I decided that if I couldn't do it naturalistically I'd be completely abstract with just a blue backcloth and six chairs.

Frayn, interviewed by Ray Connolly,
'Playwrights on Parade', *Sunday Times*, 27 Jan. 1980

It's the only play I've ever managed to start with a funny scene. Everything else is scene after scene ploddingly set up. In *Clouds* people did see this very simple joke — two people are very outgoing to each other because they think their interlocutor is foreign and therefore everything's very different. They can put on a bit of a performance for each other. Then, to their horror, they discover that the other person is exactly like themselves — another middle-class citizen from England. They realize they've been embarrassing so that both withdraw into their shells and dislike each other. Every time I saw it, that scene made people laugh. . . .

At Hampstead, the first time, it got mixed reviews. The good reviews said simply that it was a funny play, about journalists, Cuba, and being abroad. But the second time, after the other reviewers had read, I suppose, Cushman in *The Observer*, the play got universally good notices and most of the reviewers talked about it in terms of the ideas — the themes of perception. . . . It's better, in some ways, if people just see them as stories, funny or picturesque or whatever, so that the ideas are absorbed unconsciously. . . .

Bold inversions do happen in life. One does sometimes radically change one's feelings as Owen does in *Clouds*. In the course of a few days people's views do shift in that kind of way because they shift in response to each other. Mara and Owen . . . the first error, they're embarrassed and withdraw from each other. They dislike each other. The first shift of feeling occurs when Mara becomes attracted to the guide — which does happen — and accordingly cheers up and becomes more attractive. This irritates Owen even further. The only really sudden change of feeling is when Owen realizes that he is drawn to Mara — that irritates everyone else. That's really the only inversion that occurs. [Ed] doesn't change his mind exactly. But having been enthusiastic he becomes sour about it. In his irritation at Owen and Mara, he becomes rather grumpy and sour in general, as does the guide who now feels rather rejected. There's not an awful lot of changes — that's just typical group dynamics, five people together for five days.

Craig Raine, 'The Quarto Interview',
Quarto, No. 4 (March 1980), p. 4, 6

In *Clouds* this imposition of ideas is at an even more fundamental level — in the very act of apprehending the world at all. Could anything be simpler — could anything be more *passive* — than opening our eyes and letting the world enter? But what these people see as they travel about the unfamiliar and ambiguous land they are visiting depends upon what they think and feel; the complication in this rationalist scheme being that what they think and feel is affected by what they see.

Frayn, 'Introduction', *Plays: One*, p. xiii

The theme of Michael Frayn's *Clouds* may best be considered in the light of two exchanges between Hamlet and Polonius. The first, concerning what might be called the cumulative effects of cumulus, demonstrated that a cloud might assume the shape, given goodwill or gullibility in the beholder, of a camel, a weasel, or a whale. The other consists of the question 'what do you read, my lord?' and the answer, concrete without being specific, 'words, words, words'. Words, like clouds, can mean anything. This is hardly a new idea, even in the theatre; indeed the theatre might be considered its natural home. Life can be presented as a continual banana-skin joke: every man the prisoner of his own preconceptions and continually stumbling over his neighbour's. . . .

Every scene is a game of cross-purposes, and the play is in fact staged by Michael Rudman as a series of games. . . . The play's many virtues do not include suspense. They do, however, include surprise. . . .

One of Mr. Frayn's achievements is to provide the first convincing love-scenes to reach our stage in years but, the play being what it is, the love presented is conditional and much undermined. . . .

Frayn's word-play is less effervescent than Tom Stoppard's, but even more acute; his view of the middle classes better humoured than Alan Ayckbourn's (and his farce accordingly less mechanically expert), but his satire even more accurate.

Robert Cushman, 'Clouds over Cuba', *The Observer*, 23 Aug. 1976

This is the first time any [West End theatre] has dared reduce a nation to half-a-dozen white chairs and a white table, surrounded by nothing but a blue cyclorama. And, of course, it works very well, whether the cast is asked to eat, drive, work on its typewriters, or simply sit and talk. More than that, it helps make Mr. Frayn's point for him, because it proves that the imagination can transform the bits and pieces of an average middle-class kitchen into a car, a hotel, a government office, a new town, or (for all we know) a camel, weasel, or whale. Reality is what we dupe ourselves into believing.

Benedict Nightingale, 'Silver Lining',
New Statesman, 10 Nov. 1978

A chamber-work, that might have seemed intolerably static in other hands, pulses with life because of Mr. Frayn's mercurial wit.

Francis King, *Sunday Telegraph*, 5 Nov. 1978

If the play had been written by an American I suspect that we should feel it to be pretty anti-British, for the two English characters are by far the silliest. . . . Though Mr. Frayn's succession of scenes inevitably loses momentum, it nevertheless has more to say about human nature than anything else he has yet written for the stage — and is unfailingly funny and kindly at the same time.

J. W. Lambert, 'Plays in Performance', *Drama*, Autumn 1976, p. 46

You know that the Cuba the journalists write about will also be an invention, telling us more about their state of mind than about the conditions of the country. What is good about the play, in fact, is that it manages to work so well on so many different levels. As a satire on government-sponsored trips it is biliously accurate, with the writers being asked to envisage glittering new communities in a pile of dust and rubble. As a portrait of sexual jealousy, it is poignantly and unerringly funny ('So unprofessional', seethes Shorter as he watches the novelist canoodling with the handsome guide). But, above all, the play questions the whole notion of documentary truth in any form of reporting; it reminds you that the man who points the camera or wields the pen is not some unbiased, unprejudiced automaton but a fallible mortal whose excitement or boredom may be dependent on a hundred external factors.

Michael Billington, *The Guardian*, 17 Aug. 1976

One of Frayn's points is the differing ways in which we perceive things, which vary from mood to mood as much as from person to person; and another is the way sexuality dominates our behaviour. This journey of four men and a woman, every woman's dream-nightmare, begins with all the men ogling Mara, settles for a time on the guide, moves to a moment's resolution with her British colleague, and ends with the woman triumphantly beside the grinning chauffeur, the three men in various stages of defeat in the back seat. A woman might have written another outcome, but Frayn leaves his open to speculation, and my own is that Mara will not get the best of it. It is a pleasure to see what used to be called the war between the sexes explored so honestly and wittily.

Victoria Radin, *The Observer*, 5 Nov. 1978

When I first saw *Clouds* I paid insufficient attention to its title, and took it to be a wonderfully comic battle between a trio of rival reporters on a tour of Cuba. . . . The play is not a hedging piece of reportage: it is a comedy on the nature of perception, with Cuba itself . . . as an empty canvas on which the subjective impressions of each voyager are inscribed. I still experienced a slight fall in the dramatic temperature of Michael Rudman's production when the journalistic comedy gives way to a love scene in which Frayn spells out the play's essentials by allowing the couple to gaze up into the sky and read their own images into the passing clouds. But that interlude does not outstay its welcome, and the production recovers its zest in a second act of unexpected social comment and farcical violence.

Irving Wardle, *The Times*, 2 Nov. 1978

Balmoral

Play in two acts.
First production: Yvonne Arnaud Th., Guildford, 20 June 1978
(dir. Eric Thompson).
Revived: revised version, as *Liberty Hall*, Greenwich Th., London,
24 Jan. 1980 (dir. Alan Dossor; with George Cole as Skinner);
revised version, as *Balmoral*, Playhouse, Leeds, 29 Aug. 1985
(dir. John Harrison); revised version, as *Balmoral*, Bristol Old Vic,
8 May 1987 (dir. Leon Rubin).
Published: revised version, Methuen, 1987; in *Plays: Two*.

The setting of Michael Frayn's new play Liberty Hall *at the Greenwich Theatre is Balmoral Castle in 1937, all antlers and tartan linoleum, with an electric fire perched on a tea-chest in the marble fireplace; for the Revolution happened in England, not Russia, and Balmoral is a writers' home run by the Ministry of Works (the state painters are kept at Sandringham). And so we come upon those representative 'people's writers' of the 1930s, Godfrey Winn, Warwick Deeping, and Enid Blyton, breakfasting off barley and turnip kedgeree, waited on by dour John McNab (Rikki Fulton in wellingtons, kilt, green baize apron, and cloth cap), and chivvied by Mr. Skinner, the fussy administrator who rabbits on about dockets, breakfast vouchers, and the petty larceny of McNab: the legs of the billiard table have disappeared overnight. The fourth writer in residence, Hugh Walpole, has also disappeared overnight. The Inspector is expected; Hugh Walpole must be produced at all costs. Somebody must be Hugh*

Walpole. That is all you need to know for the moment. After a slowish start, the play escalates into a sequence of substitutions and mistaken identities which gives George Cole as Mr. Skinner (and sometimes as John McNab) and Rikki Fulton in triplicate as John McNab, as Hugh Walpole being himself, and as John McNab being Hugh Walpole, multiple opportunities to be themselves impersonating someone they have it in for. Hugh Walpole can never have been so funny in his lifetime, which in this play is brutally curtailed, since he has a heart attack at an inopportune moment. A corpse is always good for a laugh, and his is briefly propped up to deceive the Inspector — who is really a journalist from capitalist Russia — and then consigned to Godfrey Winn's cabin trunk. Rikki Fulton's parallel identity as McNab is achieved by pantomime-style stage-mechanics which work as slickly as a banana-skin. . . . The second act is played with all the characters getting drunker and drunker — a 'liberating' device that is not so boring here as it seemed in Donkeys' Years. *It gives Enid Blyton a chance to let her hair down; she has been writing 'curiously obscure erotic verse' under duress, since her children's stories are banned by the state. Godfrey Winn, a balding faun in tartan knee socks, has a good cry about his dear mother, as does the emotional Russian; and Warwick Deeping's, in a silver photograph frame, is passed from hand to hand. . . . There is a lot of slapstick business involving pig-weighing scales, pyjama bottoms, a two-penny stamp stuck on the bottom of a champagne bucket, and who's going to bag Walpole's bedroom (the only warm room in the castle).*

Victoria Glendinning, 'Author, Author, Author',
Times Literary Supplement, 1 Feb. 1980

[At Guildford] it didn't turn out at all as I expected. The basic situation (about there having been a revolution in England and not in Russia) I allowed to trickle out very slowly in the course of Act I — thinking that the thing to do was to establish *these* people in this particular place and *then* very gradually let it be known what was causing the anomalies in the situation. The result was just incomprehensible. People sat there through Act I quite unable to follow what was going on.

Frayn, interviewed by Craig Raine, 'The Quarto Interview',
Quarto, No. 4 (Mar. 1980), p. 3

[At Guildford in 1978] it was terrible. I withdrew it and completely rewrote it. The new version was done in the following year at the Greenwich Theatre, under a new title: *Liberty Hall*. It was a wonderful production, one of the best I have ever had. . . . The next night, as so often happens after a particularly good first preview, the show was down. . . . I don't think my memory is overdramatizing the occasion when I recall that the evening passed in absolute silence, with not a single laugh from beginning to end. This was the press night, and the reviews next morning were lacklustre. . . . As the run went on we got quite a lot of our laughs back, though we never quite recovered that first wild glory. But any prospects of further life for the play had been killed by the press night. . . .

I subsequently rewrote the play yet again, and then again, and it's been produced once or twice since. But it's never had much success. I see now, with hindsight, that it couldn't possibly work, because it's based upon an entirely abstract notion, a pure counterfactual — a past that never happened, that never *could* happen. This is of course the subject of the play — the idea that things could be other than they are, the notion of imposing a fiction upon reality, of making the dead alive, of reading servitude as liberty — and of altering reality in the process. In the first place I think this was simply too oblique to grasp — people were heard coming out at the end saying to each other in bewilderment, 'But there *wasn't* a revolution in this country. . . .' And in any case it's not a possible basis for farce. Farce, I now realize, has to be rooted in immediately believable reality. . . . *Balmoral*, I now realize, was doomed from the first by a fundamental conceptual error. It was a Titanic searching for its iceberg. In which case how could it have made people laugh that once . . . ?

'Introduction', *Plays: Two* (1991), p. viii-xi

The piece has set up a political scheme for strictly farcical purposes. It all hinges on the return and death of Walpole, and the substitution of McNab, the booted butler, for the great man. . . . Explosions of group action are separated by long periods of mute embarrassment as McNab drunkenly holds the floor.

Irving Wardle, *The Times*, 25 Jan. 1980

This middle section of the play is golden, but the sequel is forced and the preamble protracted. The mechanism hangs heavy; it is difficult to believe in science-fiction when it already hasn't happened. Besides, the three supporting writers become positively irritating, so little is done with them; and it is far from clear when they participate in the charade, since they all dislike the Balmoral Warden, whose face they are being asked to save.

Robert Cushman, The Observer, 27 Jan. 1980

How would our scribes and scribblers have conducted themselves under Stalinism? That's the question Michael Frayn conjures out of his thinking cap, jinks and wittily juggles with, but does not altogether answer. . . . The naming of names gives the covert accusations of apathy and avarice a certain scandalous frisson, yet doesn't take us as far as it might. What I, for one, wanted to know was what these pliant wordsmiths were actually writing, where and how they lived when not toiling at Balmoral, how they squared aspiration with achievement, conscience with compulsion. What Mr. Frayn does instead is use their unspoken fear of an offstage firing-squad to generate some traditional tensions and, out of them, belly-laughter. . . . This is a sophisticated drollery, an educated amusement.

Benedict Nightingale, 'Scribes', New Statesman, 1 Feb. 1980

Is it an immensely artful mis-matching of farce-form with recalcitrant content, or just a stunning series of own goals? . . . Farce reduces human beings to objects buffeted by the impersonal whims of chance. Marxism pictures human destiny as a farce with a happy ending: whole eras and classes knocked down like dithering skittles by History's benign, unerring bowl. Does the author want to highlight this symmetry? Not, it seems, a bit. What Mr. Frayn demonstrates is that, if the Revolution had happened here, some (perhaps saving) laziness and cynicism in our writers would have prevented them from becoming the fast-propelled robots of the state. This accounts for, without justifying, the very stock, off-the-peg elements of the plot. Only these, it is implied, would be likely to jolt this dozy crew into brisk automatism. . . .

There are some very good literary in-jokes, but the play sabotages itself by having no real representative of fanatical Soviet thinking. This spoils the funniest moments. Even the hilarious sequence in which Trisha, Kochetov's official guide and gushing Walpole-freak, tries to discuss a footling point of character motivation with first the corpse of Walpole and then the mute, disguised McNab, completely loses its edge. Trisha is supposed to represent unregenerate fan worship and the freedom (officially forfeited in Soviet thinking) to love bad writing and to identify with sentimentalized fantasy figures. But since nobody ever puts the Soviet view of literature at all forcefully, Trisha does not come across as the naughty renegade she should.

Paul Taylor, The Independent, 16 May 1987

Make and Break

Play in two acts.

First production: Lyric Th., Hammersmith, 12 Mar. 1980, transferred to
Haymarket Th., 24 Apr. 1980 (dir. Michael Blakemore; with Leonard
Rossiter as Garrard, Prunella Scales as Mrs. Rogers, James Grout as
Olley, and Peter Blythe as Prosser).

First American production: Playhouse, Wilmington, 28 Mar. 1983,
transferred to Kennedy Centre, Washington, 7 Apr. 1983
(dir. Blakemore; with Peter Falk as Garrard).

Television: BBC-2, 7 June 1987 (dir. Michael Darlow; with Robert
Hardy as Garrard, Judi Dench as Mrs. Rogers, Ronald Hines as
Olley, and Martin Jarvis as Prosser).

Published: Eyre Methuen, 1980; in *Plays: One*.

*High in a hotel in Frankfurt, in a suite given over to a display of
movable British walls, [Frayn] looks at the business of building
and trading. Opening as he means to go on — with three
salesmen, a torrent of words and the displayed walls and doors
falling open and forming new shapes for the benefit of three
customers — he narrows the interest down to the entrance of
John Garrard, a hyperactive, unstoppable salesman. . . . Garrard
is a businessman with a sense of competition so heightened that
he cannot enter a doorway without clambering on a chair to
discover who manufactured the door. He exists only as a salesman, questioning people cleverly, but almost unconsciously,
about their innermost desires as if he were shaking their hands.
Even while seducing the adoring secretary, so wisely portrayed
by Prunella Scales, he is sure to examine her shoe for its label,
inquire about her arrangements with her lover, and ask her for a
lesson on Buddhism, never forgetting that his key to a break-
through into the Eastern European market nestles in her hand-
bag. Bombs may shake the hotel, and they do, death may come
calling, and it does, but while all his staff wonder what it is that
motivates him, knowing that it is not money, or the love of work,
he rolls relentlessly forward like a human juggernaut.*

Ned Chaillet, *The Times*, 19 Mar. 1980

Make and Break is about how we all compulsively exploit the
possibilities of the world around us — about how we eat it — how we

have to eat it — how we transform it into food and clothes and housing, and of course lay it waste in the process. Is Garrard more monstrous than the rest of us? If he seems so, isn't it because he lacks our saving hypocrisy — because he fails to dissemble the appetites that we all have, that we all must have if we are to survive? . . . Garrard makes walls and doors. Could anyone really think I am advocating a world without walls and doors? All I'm trying to show is what they cost.

Frayn, 'Introduction', Plays: One, p. xiii

[Garrard's] way of coping with his feelings [about Olley's death at the end] is to get on with the work. Isn't that deeply characteristic of all human beings? . . . Most human beings weep, then go back to work, and Garrard won't weep. But everyone goes back to work. . . . He's an exaggeration of certain things which are normal. . . . He won't go through the normal processes — of saying what a nice bloke Olley was, taking a day off work, being upset — he just wants to get on with the work. But I would think that means he's very frightened of death. He's frightened of the machine stopping, the structure running out. I think the sight of old Olley's dead body gave him a hell of a shock. He goes out of the room for a bit to fix it. When he comes back, he's got a face for the world. . . . He's *frightened* and keeping fear at bay with all that activity. Indeed, when Garrard thinks he himself is dying, he's extremely frightened and behaves without any dignity. Well, he *is* a monster, certainly. But I would have thought that there's a lot of what seems monstrous in all of us.

Frayn, interviewed by Craig Raine, 'The Quarto Interview',
Quarto, No. 4 (Mar. 1980), p. 6

[Frayn] is still learning how to reconcile his sly, satiric wit with what's surely a more melancholic temperament and a bleaker outlook than is generally recognized, and *Make and Break* has its lapses both of tone and momentum; but it's a genuine attempt to deepen his work. . . . What galvanizes Garrard, the ageing whiz-kid unstoppably played by Rossiter? His life is spent manically maximizing profits for other people, and his conversion is no less hectic, all sudden U-turns and dizzying tangents.

Benedict Nightingale, New Statesman, 28 Mar. 1980

I could not help feeling once again that Frayn should check his 'how to make anything seem ridiculous in three easy sentences' ability a little more than he does. Too many easy laughs put the drive of this type of play at risk, whilst at times unbalancing the tone beyond the point of credibility. . . . The tragic ending is just saved from degenerating into tasteless farce.

Leonie Caldicott, *Plays and Players*, Apr. 1980, p. 24

Frayn uses a German trade fair as an excuse to explore an astonishing variety of themes: work as both devouring obsession and consolation for the lonely; the mystery of art and religion; and man's twin urge to both build and destroy. As he showed in *Alphabetical Order*, Frayn has the rare ability to construct farcical comedy around philosophical principles and here the laughs and the ideas effortlessly intermesh.

Michael Billington, *The Guardian*, 25 Apr. 1980

It is wretchedly constructed; old-fashioned in its views of women; relies on a surprise ending which would have suited a comedy thriller, but which left the Haymarket audience tittering and giggling with embarrassment, not being able to believe that Mr. Frayn took it seriously; depends for an interminable time at the beginning on scenic tricks and *trucs* with characters rushing in and out of opening and shutting doors without a trace of the expertise which sometimes makes trap-door exploits in pantomimes acceptable; and the principal part of the businessman so obsessed with his profession that he brings about the death of one of his colleagues is played by Leonard Rossiter with dour and dreadful monotony and morosity which most of my colleagues have mistaken for great acting.

There are, however, consolations for this dreary evening spent in the desert. At least, I can think of one. This is when Peter Blythe's light-heartedly atheistic salesman Frank Prosser, who is supposed to be fond of music as well as of girls, bursts suddenly into the Hymn to Joy in Beethoven's Ninth Symphony; and it is followed by another, again supplied by Mr. Blythe. For when the unexpected death occurs it is that of a colleague who happens to be a Roman Catholic, and then Mr. Blythe, breaking into momentary seriousness and sincerity which I do not find elsewhere in the play, half-ashamedly and with great emotional delicacy, brilliantly holding the centre of the stage, almost apologetically says that though we all know that what the dead man believed is nonsense, nevertheless it gave to him a kind of rest and peace which, he implies, they themselves have not got. . . .

Rossiter does not play Garrard as if the man were on the verge of a nervous breakdown. He plays him as if a nervous breakdown were his natural home. This destroys all satire and, worse than that, is intolerably boring.

Harold Hobson, 'Hobson's Choice', *Drama*, July 1980, p. 35

Frayn writes as if he were Ben Jonson let loose in the world of the export market: his characters are driven, as if by some obscure electronic passion, towards something that turns out to be the pursuit of unhappiness. But what marks Frayn off from the Jonsonian breed is a sense of appalled compassion. You can tell that he feels for these people because he has given them lives outside the shark-pool in which we observe them. . . . The play is full of pain, ruthless observation, and a sense of humour which is sardonic, lunatic, and warm. . . . Garrard is one of those leaders of men who inspire puzzled and reluctant affection because they are both dynamic and defenceless: their huge energy spurts from a body which can look helpless because it seems entirely empty of humanity. Rossiter carries his sleek head with a sort of ferrety fury, full of innocent, almost likeable malevolence. It is a mesmerizing performance.

John Peter, *Sunday Times*, 23 Mar. 1980

I have never been too sure about Michael Frayn's writing in the past. Yes, it is funny, in parts, but it all too often seems to me to have something too determined and strenuous about it, like a funny uncle at a children's party — you laugh more often out of politeness, on account of all the work he is putting into it, than because you are really, unaffectedly amused. In *Make and Break* he seems to have largely escaped this problem. . . . The play has more sheer dramatic drive than any of Frayn's previous plays. It works in many ways as a bit of a confidence trick: all the way through he holds out to us promises that sooner or later we are going to get to the root (or at least a root) of the mysterious John Garrard's character. . . . In the end Frayn never tells us or even gives us much of a hint. But he does keep us happily guessing throughout a longish evening. . . . There is still some residual evidence that Frayn is not quite a natural playwright — the set pieces, like Prunella Scales's perfectly delivered analysis of just why and how she likes her work, her life being built on happy expectation of coming to a conclusion, tend to stick out from their context — but the overall structure is right.

John Russell Taylor, 'London', *Drama*, July 1980, p. 41

Noises Off

Play in three acts.
First production: Lyric Th., Hammersmith, 23 Feb. 1982, transferred to Savoy Th., 31 Mar. 1982 (dir. Michael Blakemore; with Paul

Eddington as Dallas, Patricia Routledge as Otley, Nicky Henson
as Lejeune, and Michael Aldridge as Mowbray).

First American production: Brooks Atkinson Th., New York, 11 Dec.
1983, followed by tour to Chicago and Toronto (dir. Blakemore;
with Brian Murray as Dallas, Dorothy Loudon as Otley, Victor
Garber as Lejeune, and Douglas Seale as Mowbray).

Film: released 1992 (adapted by Marty Kaplan; dir. Peter Bogdanovich;
with Michael Caine as Dallas and Carol Burnett as Otley).

Published: Methuen, 1982; revised ed., 1983; in *Plays: One.*

---

*It has as its first act a pastiche of traditional farce; as its second
a contemporary variant on the formula; as its third, an elaborate
undermining of it. The play opens with a touring company dress-
rehearsing* Nothing On, *a conventional farce. Mixing mockery
and homage, Frayn heaps into this play-within-a-play a hilarious
mêlée of stock characters and situations. Caricatures — cheery
char, outraged wife, and squeaky blonde — stampede in and out
of doors. Voices rise and trousers fall. There are frenetic
undressings, dressing-ups, and dressing-downs. All of this
periodically halts as the rehearsing cast fluff lines and muff
moves. Stepping out of the stereotypes they are playing, they
reveal themselves as another set of stereotypes: muzzy old
trouper, dimwit ingénue, self-dramatizing show-stopper. Just
enough emerges about their inter-relationships to suggest that
they themselves are wobbling on the brink of the clandestine
scamperings of farce. The play's second act splendidly propels
them through such motions. In a master-stroke, Frayn twists his
set around. We witness the start of* Nothing On *again: but, this
time, from behind the scenes as it is performed at a mid-week
matinee. The doors of the set open and slam with the familiar
lunatic rapidity, but everything is now inverted. With embers of
the cast manically at odds, it is backstage that the comedy is
really fast and furious. Behind the scenes, things run crazily
truer to farcical type than in the play that is being performed out
front to a tiny audience of OAP's ('There's quite a crowd at the
front of the back stalls', the anaemically hopeful ASM has
murmured in worried encouragement). Having parodied a farce,
then brilliantly engineered his own, Frayn finally sabotages one.
The touring play, in the last act, is on its last legs. Behind-scenes
bile and booziness spill sloppily on to the stage. The set of*

Nothing On, *as we start to watch its first scene again, is the familiar framework of doors, french windows, stairs. But the play's shape is surreally pushed askew by lack of control. Demonstrating how farce depends on precision, clockwork punctuality of exits and entrances, Frayn carefully lets things become unsynchronized until the play skids into a pile up of disastrous collisions, buckled business, and wrecked lines. . . .*

Frayn's most skilful move, however, has been to hit upon a present-day equivalent to the social world of Feydeau, to whom *Noises Off* pays much muted tribute. . . . Frayn's actors, trying to sustain a performance with such doomed desperation, are the descendants of Feydeau's bothered bourgeoisie gamely struggling to keep up a decent front.

Peter Kemp, 'Mixing Mockery and Homage',
Times Literary Supplement, 5 Mar. 1982

[The idea occurred to Frayn when he watched his *The Two of Us* from the wings.] It was funnier from behind than in front, and I thought 'One day I must write a farce from behind.' I didn't know if actors would even be able to perform it. If I could have thought of a way to write a program for the second act, I would have learned to use a computer. Instead, I just had to try to remember where all nine actors and all the characters in *Nothing On* were at every moment. I often felt that I had come to the end of the bytes in my brain, that I had exceeded the capacity of my memory store.

Frayn, interviewed by Denise Worrell,
'Viewing a Farce from Behind', *Time*, 30 Jan. 1984, p. 70

It's about an anxiety everyone has, that he may make a fool of himself in public, that he may not be able to maintain his persona, that the chaotic feelings inside may burst out, that the whole structure may break down. I suspect people are seeing the kind of disaster they fear may happen to them, but one that's safely happening to these actors. They're discharging fear and anxiety in a way that doesn't hurt.

Frayn, interviewed by Benedict Nightingale,
'Michael Frayn: the Entertaining Intellect',
New York Times Magazine, 8 Dec. 1985, p. 128, 133

Noises Off is more a Freudian play than a Wittgensteinian play, about things coming out from behind the woodwork. . . . Embarrassment is a very deep emotion, something that many people fear. *Noises Off* is about embarrassment; it's about actors trying to fend off their appalling embarrassment at being unable to go on, of being unable to continue, and that is a problem in life for all human beings, of struggling on and trying to keep their act together. . . . When I was younger, I was consciously trying to imitate Feydeau, though I don't now. In fact, when I first wrote *Noises Off*, I had the company doing a Feydeau play. But afterwards I thought that Feydeau would be rather remote for an English touring company; they would probably be doing an English sex farce. So I changed the play within the play, though I was rather attached to the Feydeau pastiche in the earlier version of the play.

> Frayn, interviewed by John L. DiGaetani,
> *A Search for a Postmodern Theater*, p. 77-8

[For New York] I have in fact changed four phrases in the text to make them more comprehensible to American ears. I also made a few small cuts and improvements, but all of these have now been incorporated into the version playing in London. Michael Blakemore directed both productions in as similar a way as any two different productions ever can be directed. There was no pressure to modify this from either the pre-opening audiences or the American producers. . . . Three of this really quite outstanding company are in fact British, and two more have acted for long periods in Britain. They sound as British as it is possible to be.

> Frayn, 'When a Transatlantic Tin Ear Sees *Noises Off*',
> letter to *The Guardian*, 21 Dec. 1983

The people in *Noises Off* are very brilliant caricatures — very recognizable, very true, and quite thin. The energy derives from the situations. That is why a farce often has a quiet first act. In *Noises Off*, it's at least quieter than the other two acts. That's because it takes time to lay down the explanatory material that will produce situational crises later.

> Michael Blakemore, interviewed by Nan Robertson,
> 'Precision that Makes Chaos Funny',
> *New York Times*, 16 Dec. 1983, Sec. III, p. 3

The joke is on us — an audience who wouldn't be caught dead at a sex farce laughs its head off at this one. My laughter finally died because Frayn fails to make his actors more than the dimmest stereotypes.

> Victoria Radin, *The Observer*, 28 Feb. 1982

Anyone who has ever rehearsed and performed a play will recognize how much truth and observation underlies its farcical caperings to make them acceptable and believable for all their patent absurdity.

> Peter Roberts, *Plays and Players*, Apr. 1983, p. 28

Frayn's apotheosis of the farce form is almost too much of a good thing: inventiveness verges on fussiness. Director Michael Blakemore's intricately choreographed confusions could do with pruning, and since Frayn's still unable to resolve the brilliant set-pieces [despite changes between Hammersmith and the transfer to the Savoy], the last act emerges as a perfunctory truncation of a series of dazzling revue sketches. The play-within-a-play theme recalls Pirandello less than Bottom's rude mechanicals. . . . Who's complaining? Certainly not the hysterical audiences.

Martin Hoyle, *Event*, 8 Apr. 1982

Act II of *Noises Off*, both as written by Mr. Frayn and staged by Michael Blakemore, is one of the most sustained slapstick ballets I've ever seen. . . . Besides being an ingeniously synchronized piece of writing and performing — with daredevil pratfalls and overlapping lines that interlock in midair — Act II of *Noises Off* is also a forceful argument for farce's value as human comedy. Perhaps nothing could top it, and Act III doesn't always succeed.

Frank Rich, *New York Times*, 12 Dec. 1983, Sec. III, p. 12

A second viewing . . . confirms several things. That it is easily the funniest modern farce since Shaffer's *Black Comedy*. That it is not just a facile romp but an elegantly sustained joke about the fragility of theatrical illusion. And that it is very much a company play, in which any one of the nine speaking characters may, at different times, come to seem the most arresting. . . .

What is fascinating about the new cast is how certain characters achieve fresh prominence. John Quayle, a tall, gangling, bony-kneed actor with clenched hair, now gives a wonderful performance as a dedicated Method performer. . . . Quayle is very skilled at walking upstairs with his trousers round his ankles or bouncing off into the wings like Jonathan Miller playing a lepidopterist; but what makes him so funny is the furrowed intellectual seriousness he brings to a man who has to have a psychological reason for taking off a grocery box. This remind us that Frayn's play is, among other things, an affectionate satire on certain theatrical types.

Michael Billington, *The Guardian*, 16 Feb. 1983

Nothing On, the play the actors who make up the cast of *Noises Off* are rehearsing and performing, is the quintessence of farce as prolonged foreplay: the men drop their trousers, the housekeeper drops her aitches, and the pretty ingénue runs on and off stage in her underwear. This is the comedy of *coitus* guaranteed by the genre always to be *interruptus* and of fornication predestined to fail, a tantalizing naughtiness of adulterous intentions always reassuringly thwarted, thereby preserving farce's sharp division between the immorality of intention and the morality of accomplishment. Around it, Frayn weaves the far funnier drama of the actors' own world turning into farce. . . . The action of such farce, always accelerating onwards its terminal velocity of *prestissimo agitato* as the characters skitter in and out of the half-a-dozen obligatory doors of the permanent set, depends on the audience's delighted recognition of the dangers of performance, the tense risk that this time the actors' timing will go awry. The actors' skill underlines the risks, draws attention to them precisely to demonstrate that this time, as on every night of the run, one door will swing shut exactly as another door on the other side of the stage swings open. The pleasure of performance far outweighs the pleasures of the play, the acting being only a pretext for the exhilaration of pure technique.

Peter Holland, *Times Literary Supplement*, 24 July 1992

On the Film

Hollywood has Americanized *Noises Off*. The wretched touring company in my play have become mostly Americans, and although the play-within-the-play that they are performing, *Nothing On*, remains the dreadful British sex farce that it always was, they are opening it in Des Moines instead of Weston-super-Mare. . . . I like the Americanization. So far as I can remember, in fact, I was the one who first suggested it. It would be easier, I felt, for an American producer to set it up with an American cast, and it would be better if their struggles with British accents and style were part of the action. This policy seems to me to have paid off handsomely — the film is most perfectly cast, with super-lative comic actors. I couldn't see for the life of me how such an inher-ently theatrical confection could be made to work in the cinema, but I think Peter Bogdanovich has brought it off. There's nothing inherently implausible about the idea of American actors performing a British play — they do it all the time. . . . The director of *Nothing On* as written is plainly (to my eye, at any rate) an American. He's never been cast or played as American, though. . . . Many of the stage productions of *Noises Off* around the world have localized the entire action. In France, for instance, it was set in France, with a French company touring a French farce. No one, so far as I can recall, remarked upon it. . . .

There's also a lot to be said for increasing the distinction between the actors of *Noises Off* and the roles they are playing in *Nothing On*. In some countries a difference of exactly this sort was introduced for its own sake. . . .

Only one adjustment to American usage caused me much anguish, and that was the requirement for a happy ending. . . . I argued a good deal about this. I had not been hired to write the screenplay, and have no responsibility for the result. . . . Bogdanovich argued back forcefully and intelligently. The play had in effect ended happily in the theatre, he suggested, when the real actors came out all smiles for their curtain calls. Then again, in a film the audience empathized much more with the characters. . . . American audiences, I was assured, didn't want to find they'd spent the last hour or two watching a bunch of *losers*. . . . In the end I had to concede that *Nothing On* just possibly might have taken Frank Rich's fancy, and made it to Broadway. Nothing is certain in show business, after all.

> Frayn, 'Dangers of Living Happily Ever After',
> *The Observer*, 19 July 1992, p. 55

With a play everybody usually starts to discuss how to change things, but I wanted the opposite, to preserve as much as possible, especially everything that had worked in the theatre. Hitchcock told me that when he filmed Frederick Knott's play *Dial M for Murder*, what made it successful was its construction, and that's the same with *Noises Off*. The other main thing was the pacing. . . . Usually a film comes out at a minute a page of script, but I discovered that Hawks's *His Girl Friday* had a script 180 pages long for a 92-minute movie. So we shot 225 pages at 25 seconds a page.

> Peter Bogdanovich, interviewed by Iain Johnstone,
> 'Poised to Make a Big Noise',
> *Sunday Times*, 26 July 1992, Sec. 7, p. 7

There is little doubt that the better you know the British theatre, the better it comes alive. That glorious mixture of tat, camp professionalism, and triumph over adversity that is the hallmark of the British touring theatre — and was summed up so beautifully in Peter Yates's film adaptation of Ronald Harwood's *The Dresser* — is somewhat etiolated here by the American setting, and American performances that, however efficient, are light years away from Frayn's special knowledge of the real, home-grown thing. . . . It is a matter of playing farce with cold-eyed efficiency, rather than with the kind of inner conviction and attention to character detail that makes it truly funny. However well Bogdanovich pushes forward, you never get the feeling that these are real people, bitching each other into likely perdition. *Noises Off* is not so much a bad film as one which should probably never have been made at all.

> Derek Malcolm, *The Guardian*, 23 July 1992, p. 30

This is a preciously plotted work, and the screen stars are funny in inverse proportion to their attempts to be funny. Thus Carol Burnett is sustainingly amusing in her underlying irritation at having to perform this pathetic stuff and subtly unsubtle in her backstage pursuit of Frederick (Christopher Reeve). . . . On the other hand John Ritter over 'sit-coms' as Garry and isn't given the time — maybe the director's fault — not to finish his lines, the defining part of his role. . . . Best of all is another Brit, Denholm Elliot, in the gift role of Selsdon — 'Am I on? I thought I heard my voice.' Disney has seen fit to add a happy ending, which makes it limp a little in the last reel, but, more tellingly, reveals that the young Turks in the story department are unaware that classic farce should end in confusion, and also misread the author's attitude to actors which, in my interpretation, sliced up their foibles with quite a cutting edge.

Iain Johnstone, *Sunday Times*, 26 July 1992, Sec. 7, p. 6

See also:

Harrell, Wade, 'When the Parody Parodies Itself: the Problem with Michael Frayn's *Noises Off*', in Karelisa V. Hartigan, ed., *From the Bard to Broadway* (Lanham, Maryland: University Presses of America, 1987), p. 87-93.
Smith, Leslie, *Modern British Farce* (Macmillan, 1989), p. 168-72.

Benefactors

Play in two acts.
First production: Vaudeville Th., London, 4 Apr. 1984 (dir. Michael Blakemore; with Tim Piggott-Smith as Colin, Oliver Cotton as David, Patricia Hodge as Jane, and Brenda Blethyn as Sheila).
First American production: Brooks Atkinson Th., New York, 22 Dec. 1985 (dir. Blakemore; with Simon Jones as Colin, Sam Waterston as David, Glenn Close as Jane, and Mary Beth Hurt as Sheila).
Televised: BBC-2, 23 May 1989 (with Alan Rickman as Colin, Michael Kitchen as David, Barbara Flynn as Jane, and Harriet Walter as Sheila).
Published: Methuen, 1984; in *Plays: Two*.

The curtain rises at the Vaudeville on the sharply raked stage of a set designed by Michael Annals and Graham Brown to accommodate a scraped pine and Aga 'sixties kitchen, with four chairs round a scraped pine kitchen table, and an empty area stage left to represent the cheerless kitchen of the house opposite. A backcloth beyond shows a grey silhouette of Victorian roof-tops, and there is a vague area of wall upstage left that is lit later to reveal the metal uprights of a fence, suggesting a half-ruined house scheduled for demolition. On this acting area, alternatively bathed in light and isolated by realms of darkness, Frayn tells the story of two couples, David and Jane, and Colin and Sheila. David is a 'sixties architect working on a plan to re-develop somewhere called Basuto Road and several other streets in South East London; Jane, an anthropologist by train-ing, runs the house and family and takes round questionnaires. Colin works on a magazine and spends the evenings compiling a fairly fatuous encyclopedia, farming out articles to friends and children, and Sheila is a State Registered Nurse, apparently reduced to incompetence by her husband's derision. The play covers a period of fifteen years, and turns on the attitudes of all four to the new high-rise development. Basuto Road, it is clear from the outset, is ripe for development, and Frayn proceeds to develop it with characteristic flair and imagination. It is, impli-citly, a tribal homeland for the good people of South London; in conversation round the scraped pine table it soon becomes one explicitly, threatened by the cultural imperialists of North London. But Basuto Road is only the shell of a dilemma, and that dilemma is only one of a series of concentric dilemmas at the core of which is the problem of philanthropy referred to in the title. Are we helping other people when we think we are helping other people, or are we simply, as Mrs. Thatcher would recom-mend, helping ourselves?

John Wells, 'Fraynian Tricks',
Literary Review, May 1984, p. 27

The Sandboy was much more static in conception than *Benefactors*. It was about the difficulties the fortunate have in finding some philosophy which will encompass their fortune in the midst of the misfortune that they plainly see surrounds them. In *Benefactors*, I moved on to a slightly more dynamic idea about the mutual relationships between the fortunate and the unfortunate, and how they affect one another. It's also about the ambiguity of the notions of fortune and misfortune, and about how what might seem like an attempt by the more fortunate to help the unfortunate might come to be the converse — that, in fact, it's the other way around, and it might be the people who are unfortunate who help the people who are fortunate. So it's got a bit more complex over the years.

> Frayn, interviewed by David Kaufman, 'The Frayn Refrain',
> *Horizon*, Jan.-Feb. 1986, p. 35

It's a serious play, but there's some comedy in it. No *Noises Off*, no business with doors, nobody falling downstairs. It's a play about helping people and being helped. . . You don't take two years to write it, find four fine actors and a fine director, and then sum it up impromptu over lunch.

> Frayn, interviewed by Mandrake,'Frayn Refrains from the Farce',
> *Sunday Telegraph*, 11 Mar. 1984

There's a bit of me in that impatience [Colin] has, and that feeling I found in myself when I was a columnist, that as soon as something appears above ground, I must knock it down.

> Frayn, interviewed by Benedict Nightingale,
> 'Michael Frayn: the Entertaining Intellect',
> *New York Times Magazine*, 8 Dec. 1985, p. 133

[The New York] version brings out more strongly the feelings and relationships of the characters, and also the narrative. That has something to do with the audience. Americans seem much more amused by the twists and turns of the plot. All humorous writing is detached. What makes it comic is a refusal to be involved with the feelings of the characters. There is rather less of that approach in *Benefactors*.

> Frayn, interviewed by William A. Henry III,
> 'Tugging at the Old School Ties', *Time*, 27 Jan. 1986, p. 67

The play was also about a change which has occurred in Europe, and I think in America as well, since the 'sixties, and a shift from the feeling that we could actually change society, which I believe was the commonly accepted wisdom at the time by most people. I think that view has largely disappeared, and we are more pessimistic now. . . . *Benefactors* is actually charting the new feeling. I don't think this new pessimism is terminal; things will change back. In the play itself, the positions of the characters are beginning to shift back again. . . . My play is not really about Le Corbusier; it's about British architects of the period. Some of them believed very passionately in high-rise buildings; others didn't but were forced to build high because that was government policy. The government assumed that this was the answer to problems and forced architects to build high. . . . One of the men in *Benefactors*,

Colin, certainly feels jealous of David though I'm not sure David is ever jealous of Colin.

Frayn, interviewed by John L. DiGaetani,
A Search for a Postmodern Theater, p. 76, 78-80

It seemed to me essential that it move like a movie, very quickly. The tail end of one scene provides an ironic comment on the first line of the next scene. . . . What happened was what I hoped would happen, which is that the American cast, not knowing or particularly caring about the nuances of social position in England and where these people are coming from, would simply examine it in terms of situations, emotional content, the ups and downs of the characters. . . . What the play is saying was not really picked up in England, or at least was not seen as being central. It's a very important play, in that it sums up the dilemma of our time — which is that so many of the political solutions and attitudes which we hoped would work to improve things have in fact proved somewhat moribund, and people don't know in which direction to put their good will any more. If you're a person of good will — and the play is not incidentally called *Benefactors* — where can you turn?

Michael Blakemore, interviewed by Leslie Bennetts,
'Michael Blakemore Talks about His Second Frayn Play',
New York Times, 30 Dec. 1985, Sec. III, p. 13

Through this *intime* little *menage à quatre*, Frayn investigates the terrain of fifteen years of friendship, marriage, the changing patterns of architecture, social responsibility, and the metaphysics of the human personality. In the end, it's not Frayn's ambition that lets him down, but the sheer implausibility of his characters that defies belief. And neither the combined sleight of hand of the actors, nor director Michael Blakemore, can invest them with sufficient interest or credibility, to make an evening spent in their company seem anything other than misplaced.

Carole Woddis, *City Limits*, 13 Apr. 1984

We don't — as in Chekhov or Ibsen — identify with or care for the characters. It's all too discreetly distanced, too much a presentation of NW cultural imperialism, a diet of Posy Simmonds and Marc's Stringalong strips.

Giles Gordon, *The Spectator*, 14 Apr. 1984

The play becomes more engaging as it goes on because these public elements begin to impinge. But Mr. Frayn holds back, concentrating to the end on the ironies implicit in the title. Doing good and do-gooding are different things. They are confused by David and Jane. . . . Frayn is such a good writer that nothing he produces can be without some saving grace, in this case the heavily ironic commentary upon personal motivations that result in undesired but morally preferable ends.

> Michael Coveney, *Financial Times*, 5 Apr. 1984

Like Frayn's *Clouds* rather than his *Noises Off*, this is a play about what people look for in life and then about what they find there; it's a play about the tyranny of the helpless, the inevitability of change, and the fact that in the end we are no better at human planning than we are at town planning. . . . In the last fifteen minutes, Mr. Frayn gets himself into his usual trouble with endings, which is essentially that he always seems to have mislaid them somewhere around the beginning of Act Two. . . . Like Stoppard's *The Real Thing* and Pinter's *Betrayal*, it may well be another example of the word-playing English dramatists of the 1960s getting back to emotional basics, but it is the most literate explanation of how we got to here from there that I have heard in a very long time.

> Sheridan Morley, *Our Theatre in the Eighties* (1990), p. 86

People can be roughly divided between those who build up their fellows, those who pull them down, and those who are inertly willing to submit to either of these processes. In Michael Frayn's *Benefactors*, David, an architect, and his wife, Jane, belong to the first of these categories; Colin, a second-rate journalist, belongs to the second, and his wife, Sheila, belongs to the third. . . . Frayn has some wonderfully perceptive things to say about the way in which people can be kind only to be cruel; of how to need to be needed by others can be a dependence quite as enslaving as to need others; and of how love or even liking is not necessarily a prerequisite of friendship. None of these four people is simple; and one of the fascinations of the evening is the cunning way in which Mr. Frayn gives a slight turn now to this one and now to that, so that the whole nexus of relationships suddenly undergoes a transformation.

> Francis King, *Sunday Telegraph*, 8 Apr. 1984, p. 16

Benefactors is a seriously amusing four-hander which takes Frayn away from the richer emotional resourcefulness of (in my opinion) his best play to date, *Make and Break*, and into the patterning of couples more familiar in Ayckbournland. It is, for him, an excessively neat, neo-classical sort of piece which draws on only a fraction of his imaginative range. . . . Something quite delicate is being said about men, women, and change — men believing they effect it, women knowing they cannot — but the real problem with the play is simply that the men remain shadows and only the women come to life.

> Michael Ratcliffe, *The Observer*, 8 Apr. 1984

The central idea is apparent. . . . Identities, purposes, relationships, no less than housing schemes, can be 'constructions', often built on foundations other than those they are thought to have. David and Jane are complacently conscious of how they have 'redeveloped' Colin and Sheila, but are less aware of how their own confidence has rested on a sense of superiority to Colin and Sheila's apparent helplessness. It is Colin, most knowing and least attractive of the characters, who sees this latter irony and exploits it ruthlessly, upsetting the psychological base David and Jane require and inducing a state in which they will 'pull each other down'. . . . The mobile and resourceful stagecraft, so evident in *Noises Off*, works somewhat equivocally in the new play. Frayn repeatedly freezes the action, allowing characters to step out of it to offer confidential or ironical comment, so that we are, as it were, constantly shifting between an onstage and a backstage view of things, in the manner of *Noises Off*. It is dexterously done, but it concentrates attention on the dramatic foreground, on a theatrical wit matching the verbal one, to the detriment of the searching, reflective vein the play is clearly meant to have. The gestures towards moral speculation — Colin's talk of 'light' and 'dark' — are clumsy; the characters never quite 'live' beyond the special preoccupations of the play; and the whole public aspect of David's scheme receives in fact very sketchy treatment. . . . The cast and Michael Blakemore's direction steer a shrewd course between easy satire — David and Jane as mere 1960s trendies — and, despite one reference to *The Master Builder*, the Ibsenesque. . . . The outstanding performance, though, is Brenda Blethyn's Sheila. A quivery mixture of vulnerability, muddle, and opportunism, she yet rises to curiously uncontradictory moments of steadiness and lucidity. Cocooned inside another couple's life, she finds herself, almost inadvertently, affirming that the reason for the world's perplexity and inertia is that people do not know what they want — they want to be told what they want. Thus in one breath she not only analyzes her own predicament — in attaching herself to David and Jane she has been given her involuntary desire — but diagnoses the malaise of domestic architecture.

Graham Swift, 'Domestic Architecture',
Times Literary Supplement, 27 Apr. 1984, p. 466

Blakemore's staging brings out all the gentler qualities of Glenn Close, an actress who can be abrasive, and an impressive range of muted hues in the mousey neighbour of Mary Beth Hurt, an actress whose subtlety has sometimes been eclipsed by an ingénue squeaky voice. Simon Jones is icily competent but monotonous as the antagonist, leaving too much drive to be supplied by Sam Waterson as the idealist in Michael Frayn's play. Energy Mr. Waterson has in abundance, and the role is complemented by his singular personality: a blend of rock-ribbed integrity, adolescent ebullience, and guileless manliness.

Holly Hill, *The Times*, 10 Feb. 1986

This prismatic work circumscribes the disillusionment of an era, no less American than English, in which grandiose dreams of a universally benevolent democracy died. . . . In favour of benefaction but despairing of its attainment, Mr. Frayn aches for all four characters and for the unseen inhabitants of Basuto Road. The engineering term 'progressive collapse' — a potential calamity in high-rise structures — carries a sad double meaning. . . . The evening's chipper ending, in which survival and wisdom prove to be life's pyrrhic victories, is about as happy as that of *The Seagull*. . . . The imagery of the opening monologue — with its delicate play of clouds and sunlight, present and past — establishes the kaleidoscopic method used throughout.

Frank Rich, *New York Times*, 23 Dec. 1985

There's not a hell of a lot more to act in *Benefactors* than sang-froid and dialect. Michael Frayn is already being compared with Chekhov, whom he has translated and adapted. But this is to confuse a journalist with a poet. . . . It is still the work of an artificer rather than an artist. An editorialist by nature, Mr. Frayn appears to have written a lead article about the evils of social engineering — and it is nice to welcome a play with some kind of public dimension. But the piece is really another story of marital treachery. . . . The English are apparently becoming obsessed with infidelity dramas about the woes of exchanging wives and husbands, a subject that originated in the plays of Noel Coward.

Robert Brustein, *Who Needs Theatre?*
(New York: Atlantic Monthly Press, 1987), p. 217

Look Look

Play in two acts.
First production: Aldwych Th., London, 30 Mar. 1990 (dir. Mike Ockrent; with Stephen Fry as Keith, Margaret Courtenay as Joan, and Robin Bailey as Quentin).
Published: Methuen, 1990.

In Look Look, *[Frayn] now advances the theory that the audience may be more interesting than what it's watching — a chancy proposition that, as it turns out, proves all too convincing. The playgoers of various ages and stations who stare out at us, watching an invisible play, are united in their indifference to the art of drama. Joan and Helena, a dragon and her repressed daughter on an obligatory night out, are apprehensive that the play may contain 'language' or nudity ('Chap's loosening his tie now', points out the indignant mum). Charles and Amanda are City and Sloane types married to other people; she is trying to keep his hand off her knee while he is calculating how long they will have in the taxi. Reginald and Eileen are hapless out-of-towners, dragging their boy-crazy teenage daughter on a miserable birthday treat. Lee, a blank-faced youth who would rather listen to his Walkman, is accompanied by Quentin, the silver-haired, silver-tongued drama teacher who hopes to initiate him into something more than an appreciation of thespian matters. In the back row are Bobbie and Merrill, an elderly American couple who are respectively starstruck and gaga. This unholy company is presided over by Keith, the unhappy spectator at the 147th performance of his play, to whom every latecomer, every crinkled sweet paper, is an arrow through his heart. Granting Frayn the licence to have his dizzy dozen chatter away undeterred by presumably hundreds of invisible playgoers, one wonders how he will create connections and involvements among them. One leaves for the interval wondering still. . . . The rest of the act is taken up with mild and predictable jokes about wrong seats, coughing, nervous seducers, and near-sighted usherettes. . . . In the second act, the cast take the parts of actors in the play they have previously been watching, a sort of exercise in Kaufman-and-Hart meet Pirandello. In the bizarre and hysterical performance that follows, the characters, who have the same personalities and problems as the audience members, give up their inhibitions along with their seats. Guilty Amanda and squeamish Helena, in particular, go for a whisky bottle and a gun, one with lethal results. Then, hey presto, we are back in the stalls again, as the play-punters file out, harrowed or uplifted. One can't, unfortunately, count the patrons of the Aldwych among them, for, though the second act is weirder than the first, it's no more amusing.*

Rhoda Koenig, *Punch*, 27 Apr. 1990

It's about how people make sense of what they see in front of their eyes. And, conversely, how actors onstage are an audience for the audience.

> Frayn, interviewed by Heather Neill, 'A Philosopher Speaks',
> *The Times*, 17 Apr. 1990

It is very galling to get bad reviews for a play and feel they're completely unjustified. It's even more galling to get bad reviews and feel that the critics are absolutely right. . . . I knew [at the first preview] that the play didn't work, and I knew that I would spend the next fourteen days rewriting every waking moment — and that still wouldn't make it into a workable play.

> Frayn, interviewed by Robert Hewison, 'A Last Look',
> *Sunday Times*, 6 May 1990, Sec. E, p. 1

One leaves the theatre open-mouthed at the sheer awful doomed ingenuity of it all, a sort of mad free-form card-house built on a sloping mirror in a high wind.

> Hugo Williams, *Sunday Correspondent*, 22 Apr. 1990, p. 41

I just have no idea what the usually adept Mr. Frayn thought he was up to. . . . *Look Look* seems to be two acts in search of a play, but I cannot conceive any play into which Act Two could fit. . . . Some time I really would like to know exactly what Michael Frayn thought it was all about.

> John Russell Taylor, *Plays International*, June 1990, p. 23

Frayn's energy goes into tortuous ingenuity; the spectator's energy goes into trying to unscramble it. There is not much left over for laughter.

> Irving Wardle, *Independent on Sunday Magazine*, 22 Apr. 1990

For all its undoubted ingenuity, the play feels like the theatrical equivalent of one of those periodic columnists writing about the impossibility of writing a humorous column.

> Michael Billington, *The Guardian*, 18 Apr. 1990

The point, if one accepts that there is one, emerges towards the end in a courtroom drama defence of theatre. It is, we hear, a confrontation, a process of watching and being watched which (grandiloquent offstage whisper) makes us understand that the present is huge and everlasting. Which is more than can be said for the play itself, however wittily Frayn sets about the business of constructing and demolishing the conventions on which it is based.

> Claire Armitstead, *Financial Times*, 18 Apr. 1990

What does it all add up to? I for one emerged from this clotted, surreal mix with two tentative conclusions. One was that Frayn wanted to suggest that, in life as in the theatre, we are simultaneously actors and audiences: watching, being watched, and watching ourselves being watched. Another was that his dramatic imagination, formidable though it is, could have expressed that idea a bit more straightforwardly.

Benedict Nightingale,
The Times, 18 Apr. 1990

Here

Play in two acts.
First production: Donmar Warehouse, London, 29 July 1993
(dir. Michael Blakemore; with Teresa Banham as Cath, Iain Glen as Phil, and Brenda Bruce as Pat).
Published: Methuen, 1993.

[*A young couple*] *are discovered inspecting the empty bedsit that Ashley Martin-Davis has designed for the tiny Donmar stage: white doors and walls, an alcove for oddments, a small cupboard posing as a kitchenette, a larger one passing itself off as a bathroom. Should they take it, should they go elsewhere? This is what they debate in an amusing parody of the sort of terse, elliptical code couples often use:* 'It's a bit, well.' 'Whatever?' 'All the same.' 'Ah.' 'No.' 'Go on.' 'Nothing.' *By such means they muddle their way to a conclusion that neither quite likes, each wonders if the other wants, and both suddenly discover they have somehow reached. Yes, they'll take the flat. It is all very English. . . . They move into their white box and try to give some shape to their lives and exercise some control over their environment:* 'It's our piece of space, our world. We can't have things imposed upon us. We can't have things we didn't choose ourselves.' *But tell that to Brenda Bruce, playing their importunate landlady, who turns up to present them with her dead husband's favourite chair, along with a lot of gloomy memories. Tell that to Cath and Phil themselves, who are soon wrangling about the rest of the furniture, notably whether their bed, centre of their love-life, should be in the middle of the room or shunted sideways. As it turns out, their love-life has more downs than ups, largely because Bruce is an unwitting proponent of coitus interruptus, forever knocking on the door at the wrong sexual moment. Indeed, as the evening proceeds, they quarrel more and more: about his irritating speech-patterns and nose-picking habits, her Snoopy doll, his Ronald Reagan mask, and, above all, which part of the room belongs to whom. Michael Blakemore gets excellent performances from both Banham and Glen, she alternately snappish and sunny, he exasperated, apologetic, and, for a moment, despairing. By now Uncle Michael's implicit advice is painfully obvious. People, especially bright, edgy people, need more than one room if they are not to drive each other nuts. As for philosopher Frayn, he has had much to say or suggest about the vanity of trying to order lives, relationships, space, language, and, by inference, the world.*

Benedict Nightingale, *The Times*, 6 Aug. 1993, p. 30

Michael has dramatized what one might call the true present. All plays are perceived to be happening in the present, but like most literature they're written out of the remembered past. They have the shape that memory imposes on experience. This play shows the extent to which what we say is secondary to our instinctual life. In this case, our instinctual competition for space and attention. While the landlady recalls her life in the form of conventional drama, the couple are constantly improvising. It's an extraordinary drama out of tiny events, and a remarkable feat of observation.

Michael Blakemore (director), quoted by Michael Church,
'Wonders from the Fingers of Mike',
The Observer, 1 Aug. 1993, p. 47

My character has a pretty dry, astringent attitude to their behaviour, but she understands, because she's been there and done it all herself. Her feelings about young love are more 'Thank God that's all behind me' than nostalgic in any way. The play does deal with innocence and experience, but she's certainly no agony aunt – I think this play is unlike any other I've acted in because it manages to be extremely funny and human without any trace of mawkishness or sentimentality. It's funny because of the huge number of things that you instantly – sometimes very embarrassingly – recognize in it. I'm quite sure that any couples in the audience will leave saying 'That's exactly what you do!'

Brenda Bruce, quoted by Sam Willetts,
'Here and Now,' *What's On*, 4 Aug. 1993, p. 9

[The young couple] express themselves constantly in a numbing form of repeat-speak with pedantic, humourless word-play. . . . This diction, with its reiterative pseudo-comic patter, soon becomes naggingly oppressive. It leads nowhere. It establishes and reveals next to nothing. It is undramatic. It lacks theatrical point. . . . Everything is repeated more than twice. The lovers argue trivially and at enormous length over furnishings. . . . The pair are also outstandingly dull, since Frayn treats them merely as types. He is all male rationality and logic. She represents feminine emotionalism. The argumentative chatter focuses with exclusive banality on the edgy progress of their love and power relations.

Nicholas de Jongh,
Evening Standard, 5 Aug. 1993, p. 7

It's a vindictively dull scenario. A steady drip of monosyllabic questions and fudged answers create a hell of indecision as the duelling protagonists endlessly circle the real premise: just how compatible are they? . . . By denying us any outline of these people's lives – what they do, where they come from – Frayn's characters become as insubstantial as their vapid dialogue. By trying to define them purely in terms of 'here and now' we cease to care.

James Christopher,
Time Out, 11 Aug. 1993, p. 107

Although Frayn makes a skilful entertainment out of inarticulacy – and Michael Blakemore's energetic production does everything in its power to inoculate us against boredom – Cath and Phil irritate each other and boy, did they irritate me! Paying them the compliment of believing in them, I found myself thinking: haven't you got any work to do? Split up or shut up. The treat of this production is Brenda Bruce's Pat, the landlady. She appears at the door like a Cheshire cat with marmalade hair and a cheesy smile, politely intrusive, aggressively lonely.

Kate Kellaway, *The Observer*, 8 Aug. 1993, p. 51

Here is essentially about time and space: it has all the minimalist, staccato qualities of his early novels and journalism, and seems at times to have been cobbled together by an unholy alliance of Samuel Beckett and Harold Pinter. But, as usual, Frayn has his own eccentric corner of their more familiar territory. . . . *Here* is an endlessly Scrabbled wordplay about territorial imperatives and the life-cycle of a relationship, in which the participants play a series of increasingly desperate games to try and cheat the passage of time.

Sheridan Morley, *The Spectator*, 14 Aug. 1993, p. 32

READER: What's Michael Frayn's new play at the Donmar about?

CRITIC: Time, space, and life.

READER: Oh, please. Not Pseud's Corner.

CRITIC: Not at all. After all, life takes place in time and space. Otherwise it wouldn't be life. And, of course, vice versa. . . .

READER: What's the play called?

CRITIC: *Here*.

READER: Hear what?

CRITIC: No. *Here*. In this place. You see, the title itself suggests simplicity, as if to say, here we are. Life.

READER: But where is the play? What happens?

CRITIC: What happens is that things change. . . .

READER: Sounds rather sort of lean and spare for a two-hour play.

CRITIC: You might think so but you would be wrong. Everything Frayn writes, in both his novels and his plays, has to do with how things work, how people function. This play is about how love turns into marriage. How you feel both trapped and reassured. How private games acquire public rules. Frayn is conducting a laboratory experiment which hurts.

John Peter, *Sunday Times*, 8 Aug. 1993, Sec. 9, p. 17

A: Where are we?

B: We're *here* watching Michael Frayn's new play *Here* going on there.

A: But there's nothing on the stage.

B: Put a frame round nothing and it becomes a set. This is a set representing an empty room with two people, Cath and Phil, in a dramatic situation: perhaps they'll rent it.

A: They'd be at home there, they're practically invisible. They just keep repeating themselves and asking questions. Why can't they make their minds up?

B: They're starting their lives. Naturally they haven't much to say yet.

A: They might let us know where they've come from. They must have been doing something somewhere else before they came here.

B: It isn't that sort of play. It's about here and now, which as you know are primary components of deixis – the means whereby language gears itself to the speaker and receiver, and hence the basis of dramatic dialogue.

A: That's why they don't tell us who they are?

B: Exactly. Cath, Phil, and the room are a *tabula rasa*, a blank page for experience to write on. This is a philosophic comedy.

A: Is that why they can't finish a sentence or decide about anything?

B: They will, once they've decided to rent the room. . . .

A: It still sounds as if they're making it up as they go along, and never have the nerve to say yes to any idea that comes up.

B: That's how most people do live, and meanwhile the clock ticks away.
A: What is the time, by the way?
B: I wish you'd stop asking me questions.
A: I feel I've been here for a lifetime. I'm bored, I'm sick of the routine, I want to get away.
B: Michael Frayn is a wonderful comic writer, and this human comedy would have Martians rolling in the aisles, but seen at close range by you and me, the joke does seem to be on us.

Irving Wardle,
The Independent on Sunday, 8 Aug. 1993, p. 17

Blakemore's fine production expertly keeps the mood upbeat but has sufficient flexibility to accommodate moments of wistful profundity or panic such as the mysterious episode when Cath can't find Phil though he's there in the flat, or speeches like this one of Pat's, about the in-between-rows part of her marriage: 'It wasn't like anything. . . . There it was. Then there it wasn't. It doesn't last long, Phil, I'll tell you that, whatever it's like.'

Paul Taylor, *The Independent*, 6 Aug. 1993, p. 15

If you go to see *Here* expecting to see a naturalistic slice of life, you will be disappointed. It is primarily a play of ideas – more genuinely so than, say, *Arcadia* or, at another level, *The Gift of the Gorgon*. The action is tightly patterned, the language highly (and wittily) stylized. At the same time there are realistic lessons to be learned (even if sensible, intuitive Cath stands less in need of them than Phil). No one can make the world over again from scratch. We are free to choose, but not free to choose the choices that we are offered.

John Gross, *Sunday Telegraph*, 8 Aug. 1993, p. 8

In his portrait of a relationship, Frayn also successfully dramatizes a number of ontological problems: what happens when we make a decision (Cath and Phil inside one sweater try to co-ordinate their movements while looking in the mirror); in what does personal identity lie (they try opening their eyes suddenly to catch each other fixed at one moment); where does the past go (they watch time pass, counting along with the second hand of an alarm clock)? There is even a Paul Daniels-like demonstration of Berkeley's conundrum about whether someone unobserved is really there when Phil disappears behind a curtain. Michael Blakemore makes the most of these surprises and there are some high-risk bits of staging: an extended, full-frontal bout of nose-picking, some disturbing play with a mask, and well-timed grapplings and rollings. As in Frayn's previous plays (especially *Noises Off* and *Look Look*), these moments derive a good deal of their impact from their immediacy – which is what makes *Here* a proper piece of theatre rather than just an exceptionally well-written sit-com. That and the recurring swells of sadness which the play orchestrates over the passing of our lives.

Lindsay Duguid, 'Swells of Sadness',
Times Literary Supplement, 13 Aug. 1993, p. 17

b: Translations and Adaptations

The Cherry Orchard

Translation of the play by Anton Chekhov.
First production: National Th. (Olivier), London, 3 Feb. 1978 (dir. Peter Hall).
Revived: revised version, Aldwych Th., London, 24 Nov. 1989 (dir. Sam Mendes).
Published: Eyre Methuen, 1978; revised, with condensed Introduction, in Chekhov, *Plays* (Methuen, 1988).

'There is no evidence that Chekhov was himself advocating revolution. It was a time of great political upheaval, for economic and commercial reasons, when the land-owning classes were supplanted by industrialists — and that is reflected in the play. It is about things changing.' Chekhov's willingness to show 'the unexpectedness of human emotion' is, Frayn believes, one of his strengths. 'Life goes on when people's hearts are breaking.'. . .' *The Cherry Orchard* relies somewhat more on "poetry" in its loosest sense. There is a very powerful play in there, but it is more elusive than the others.'. . . The actors must have confidence in the text, but 'some lines are prickly and awkward because they are meant to be prickly and awkward'. Frayn avoids anachronisms but, like Chekhov, gives older characters slightly old-fashioned vocabulary. . . . The Russian fondness for names — pet names, diminutives, patronymics, and nicknames can be confusing for English audiences. Frayn prefers to reduce the variations. . . . There is no reason why a translation should stand for ever 'and people do expect something different from translation, a freshness, though one does hope that it may be definitive'.

Heather Neill, 'Bleak Comedy of a Changing World',
The Times, 24 Oct. 1989, p. 15

The Fruits of Enlightenment

Translation of the play by Lev Tolstoy.
First production: National Th., 14 Mar. 1979 (dir. Christopher Morahan).
Published: Eyre Methuen (1979).

Tolstoy's construction does present real difficulties in making the play work-able. I have therefore taken the liberty of changing it, by rearranging some of the material in the second half.... I like to believe that if he had written another eight drafts he might have hit upon my scheme of things.
Frayn, 'A Note on the Translation', p. xvii

Wild Honey

Freely adapted and abridged from Anton Chekhov's lengthy untitled
    script, sometimes referred to as *Platonov*.
First production: National Th. (Lyttelton), London, 19 July 1984
    (dir. Christopher Morahan).
First American production: Ahmanson Th., Los Angeles, 9 Oct. 1986,
    transferred to Virginia Th., New York, 18 Dec. 1986 (dir. Morahan).
Published: Methuen, 1984; in *Plays: Two*, 1991. [Both include full
    Introduction.]

Including *Wild Honey* in a collection of my own plays may seem to imply unjustifiable claims about the extent of my contribution to it. I decided to put it here, though, rather than in my collection of Chekhov translations, simply to avoid any possible confusion between translation and adaptation. . . . When the play was produced some playgoers, even some reviewers, credited me with (or blamed me for) the more farcical elements. They supposed, in other words, that it began as more or less pure Chekhov and finished as more or less impure Frayn. The converse (sadly) is true. Most of the liberties I took were in getting the action of the play under way with reasonable despatch. It's true that I have emphasized the farce in what follows rather than the moralizing and melodramatic elements which are also present in the original. But the farce is essentially Chekhov's own handiwork. . . . I wish I had written it, but I didn't. I merely trimmed it and fitted it all more tightly and securely together. And, of course, translated it. I shouldn't like to forego the credit for that.
Frayn, 'Introduction', *Plays: Two*, p. xiii-xiv

Frayn's editing job was clearly immense, and neatly done — up to a point. That point is where he veers into inventions of his own and where I begin to question the ethics of the whole enterprise. . . . Perhaps the 'rights' of posterity override the sensibilities of the dead artist — but not to me. Frayn, in knocking it into shape, makes it at times a parody of those masterpieces that sprang from it.

Kenneth Hurren, *Mail on Sunday*, 22 July 1984

Wild Honey falls midway between not-quite-ripe *Cherry Orchard* and less joyously noisy *Noises Off*, and is, for all its faults, the best thing Fraykov ever wrote: charming, funny, and deeply melancholy. . . . [*Platonov* is] two different plays. There is the social play, about the bankruptcy of the landed gentry, the dilettantism of the intellectuals, and the boredom of provincial life. . . . And there is the more intimate tragicomedy of Platonov, potentially a second Byron, turned village schoolmaster and reluctant Don Juan. . . . But the two plays and their variously satirical and wistful, outrageous and agonized tones, do not mesh into what was to become Chekhov's way. . . . Nor could the adaptation, however ingenious, bridge the gap without wholly discarding the Chekhovian blueprint or forgetting all Frayn has digested — from Feydeau to the theatre of the absurd — for the sake of a lost, by now inconceivable simplicity.

John Simon, 'Milking Honey', *New York*, 5 Jan. 1987, p. 49

There is plenty of deliberate farce in *Platonov*, but Frayn has made it the informing element and adhesive of *Wild Honey*. In doing so he forces us to look in the other direction at Chekhov's revered comic predecessors, Goncharov and, above all, Gogol. Distinctly Gogolian is the dizzy accumulation of events, the hint of diabolical possession and sulphur in the air, to which the text alludes, and the speed with which the cornered Platonov leaps from the window at the end like the terrified bridegroom in *Marriage*. The effect is of an old clock completely taken apart and given a new movement. It is still Chekhov, but it is also Frayn.

Michael Ratcliffe, *The Observer*, 22 July 1984

The last scene, set in Platonov's schoolhouse, is, I suspect, at least as much Frayn's as Chekhov. Its farcical comings-and-goings are closer to *Noises Off*, or *No Sex Please, We're Russian*, than to *Ivanov*. Up to this point, though, Michael Frayn's achievement is to make us feel we are present at the birth of a fresh and captivating new Chekhov discovery.

Christopher Hudson, *Evening Standard*, 23 July 1984

The advantage of a seven-hour manuscript is that you can find in it most of whatever you happen to be looking for, and Frayn was clearly looking for two things: a manic farce in the best traditions of his own *Noises Off* and, since this was a first play, some kind of guidelines to the later Chekhov. Happily the seedlings for *The Cherry Orchard* are all here. . . . There are times when Frayn seems in his adaptation to be parodying Chekhov rather than simply translating him: lines like 'Silence — somewhere a fool is being born' and 'Sometimes I miss her after lunch — so it's love' suggest an Oxbridge arts revue *circa* 1960 rather than the long-lost training ground of a master dramatist.

> Sheridan Morley, *Punch*, 1 Aug. 1984

Chekhov's play is very long, untidy and in many respects unsatisfactory. . . . Modesty prevents Frayn admitting what we now know: he has made a virtue of the play's outlandish properties, bound farcical pay-offs into both writing and stage action, altering even such major incidents as the manner of Platonov's death, and presented a tight, moving, and funny new play in four beautifully organized acts that cast equal credit on Chekhov and his adaptor. . . . The translation seems to me to manage an exact balance between ludicrous moralizing (questions of Life and Death, where are we going, and so on are played for rich laughter), physical explosion, and that familiar Chekhovian tapestry of misunderstandings, sudden tears, and stifled hopes. For the first two acts Christopher Morahan's superb production offers a familiar new play. Then the particular tone of this piece is turned to amazingly fertile advantage by Frayn. . . . The jejune incidents on and around the railway line are concentrated into freshly minted farce by an expert hand. What he could not achieve in *Noises Off* — a coherent climax worthy of the middle act — Frayn here brings off in dazzling fashion.

> Michael Coveney, *Financial Times*, 20 July 1984

Wild Honey is a very viable play. And that, in itself, justifies Frayn's reworking of it to a certain extent — but it is very different from the original, and widely different also in its intentions. For the original, for all its comedic and farcical elements, is ultimately meant to be a tragic play. . . . Frayn has turned what Chekhov certainly intended as a serious examination of Russian society around 1880 into broad and enjoyable farce. . . . Platonov, in Chekhov's original conception, was meant to embody the tragedy of the weak-willed intellectual who is unable to resist the temptations of the flesh, too idle, too much the victim of an upper-class ethos which gloried in dilettantism and a leisurely way of life (shades of the contemporary British sickness here?). In Michael Frayn's version — and in Ian McKellen's brilliantly clownish performance — he is no more than just an amusing bounder. . . . Structurally, Frayn has greatly improved on the young and inexperienced Chekhov's rather ponderous construction. Entrances and exits operate with the precision of a Feydeau farce. . . . The best thing is to forget Chekhov and see this as what it is: Feydeau set in Chekhov country.

Martin Esslin, *Plays*, Aug. 1984, p. 2

Number One

Translation and adaptation of the play by Jean Anouilh.
First production: Queen's Th., London, 24 Apr. 1984 (dir. Robert Chetwyn).
Published: Samuel French, 1985.

Three Sisters

Translation of the play by Anton Chekhov.
First production: Royal Exchange, Manchester, 11 Apr. 1985 (dir. Caspar Wrede).
First London production: Greenwich Th., 23 Mar. 1987, transferred to Albery Th., 3 June 1987 (dir. Elijah Moshinsky).
Published: Methuen, 1983; revised, with condensed Introduction, in Chekhov, *Plays*, 1988.

The Seagull

Translation of the play by Anton Chekhov.
First production: Palace Th., Watford, Nov. 1986 (dir. Patrick Mason).
Revived: Royal Shakespeare Company, Swan Th., Stratford-on-Avon, 6 Nov. 1990, transferred to Barbican Th., London, 4 July 1991 (dir. Michael Blakemore).
Published: Methuen, 1986; with condensed Introduction, in Chekhov, *Plays*, 1988.

Exchange

Translation and adaptation of the play by Yuri Trifonov.
First production: Guildhall School, Nov. 1986 (with student actors).
First professional production: Nuffield Th., Southampton, 21 Nov. 1989, transferred to Vaudeville Th., London, 19 Feb. 1990 (dir. Patrick Sandford).

Published: Methuen, 1990.

I saw the original production of *Exchange* in Moscow in 1978, and immediately asked the author's permission to translate it; not something I have been moved to do before or since. . . . It seemed to me that the play needed not just translating but a good deal of rethinking to make it workable on a British stage. After I had done a first draft I went back to Moscow and got Trifonov's consent to various changes. . . . I got Trifonov's permission to restore various sections from the original novel — mostly ones that helped to bring alive the physical reality of Moscow — and fleshed out the lives of his characters. . . . I hope all my changes have remained faithful to the spirit of the original. . . . The play can never have the same familiarity to an English audience that it does to a Russian one. But this has some advantages. It has the effect of showing us our own world at a distance, the too familiar tangle of our own existence made new and unfamiliar by being refracted through someone else's *byt*. Because in the end this is us.

Frayn, 'Introduction', p. v-xi

It is a Soviet variation on Chekhov's Andrei and Natasha: the aimlessly well-meaning husband and the self-righteously selfish wife. But it is also as though Andrei had written *Three Sisters*. Viktor is not only the narrator: the entire drama takes place inside his head. Martin Jarvis plays him like a man at the midnight of his youth, looking back on the past with a crooked, sickly smile and then embarking on another feverish replay of how his life went down the drain. . . . In Patrick Sandford's production . . . the effect is abrasively funny as well as self-lacerating. It also projects the poetry of time through a brilliantly resourceful use of the psychological present tense — which shows, say, the grandfather sitting through his own funeral and then carrying on speaking; or Viktor's reunion with a father younger than himself who leads his aged wife into a lyrical waltz, before the screech of a trolley bus drags Viktor into the present . . . .

Irving Wardle, *The Independent on Sunday*, 25 Feb. 1990

Uncle Vanya

Translation of the play by Anton Chekhov.
First production: Vaudeville Th., London, 12 May 1988 (dir. Michael Blakemore).
Published: Methuen, 1987; with condensed Introduction, in Chekhov, *Plays*, 1988.

The Sneeze

A full-length show for seven actors, comprising translations of four
    short plays by Chekhov (*The Evils of Tobacco*, *Swan Song*, *The Bear*,
    and *The Proposal*), with adaptations of four stories by Chekhov,
First production: Aldwych Th., London, 21 Sept. 1988 (dir. Ronald Eyre).
Published: Methuen, 1989; the four one-act plays also in Chekhov,
    Plays, 1988.

Chekhov wrote about eight short plays in all. I think four of them are
terrific, and the other four are not so good, though some of the other four
are sometimes done. The four that we are doing are the four everyone
does — *The Bear*, *The Proposal*, *The Evils of Tobacco,* and *Swan
Song*. . . . I've taken four short stories from about the same period
(*Drama*, *The Alien Corn*, *The Inspector General*, and *The Sneeze*) and
adapted them. Chekhov did that with several of the plays himself. *The
Wedding*, *The Anniversary*, and *Swan Song* are all adapted from short
stories, so I'm not originating the technique. . . . They are straightforward comic plays. They were done to be played in boulevard theatres
by popular comic actors. They don't have any of the enormous problems
of nuance and tone, balancing comedy and pain and so forth, that the
later plays have. They are simply straightforward comic plays. . . . I think
they're good comedies — comedies which offer a lot of opportunities to
actors, and I hope they're going to be funny.
> Frayn, interviewed by Mick Martin, 'A Not So Cosy Bear',
> *Plays International*, Sept. 1988, p. 19

The word 'Chekhovian' has been applied, with generous imprecision, to
a fair number of things in this world; but probably never, even in its
vaguest sense, to Chekhov's own one-act plays. They are in a different
mode from the four great dramas that constitute the Chekhovian in most
people's minds; they are offered not as art but as entertainment. The best
of them are (for the greater part) straightforwardly comic. . . . Chekhov's
vaudevilles are of somewhat mixed quality. . . . The four I have chosen
for this collection have solid theatrical virtues. *The Evils of Tobacco* and
Swan Song both touch upon some deeper desolation than boulevard
plays normally care to show. . . . Chekhov's designation for *The Bear*
and *The Proposal*, 'joke', is usually translated into English as 'farce.'
The term is of course as capacious as 'Chekhovian', but there is a
considerable difference between these plays and most French or English
farces. As we know the form, it usually depends upon panic, and the
panic is usually generated by guilt and the prospect of some kind of
social disgrace. The panic leads in its turn to deceit, which produces
further and yet more alarming prospects of disgrace, from which grows

ever greater panic, in a spiral known to scientists as positive feedback. There is no panic in *The Bear* or *The Proposal*, no deceit or threatened outrage. What drives these characters is a sense of outrage — of anger at the failure of others to recognize their claims, whether to money or to land or to a certain status. In their anger, it is true, they lose the ability to control their destinies or even to recognize their own best interests, just as the characters of traditional farce do in their panic. This is what these plays have in common with English and French farces — that their characters are reduced by their passions to the level of blind and inflexible machines; though this reduction is precisely what Bergson thought (implausibly, to my mind) was the common factor in all comedy. Chekhov may well have taken his vaudevilles more seriously than his offhandedness about them suggests. One of the liberties I have taken in this collection is to restore some of the humour of the earlier versions of *The Evils of Tobacco*. . . . I have also made some slight changes to *Swan Song*. . . . I recognize my presumption in adding to the world's stock of Chekhov plays, but if these adaptations intrigue a few theatregoers into reading the originals, and exploring for themselves the ever more wonderful stories that Chekhov was writing in those amazing years, then my effrontery will be more than justified.

Frayn, 'Introduction', *The Sneeze*, p. viii-xv

[Frayn's] brilliance as an adaptor can be seen in the way he has transformed a three-page story, 'The Death of a Government Official', into a side-splitting, wordless mime *The Sneeze*.

Paul Taylor, *The Independent*, 29 Sept. 1988

Their natural wit and vivacity bring home the inappropriateness of that fog of languid nostalgia that clings to the term 'Chekhovian'. Frayn, through his translations of the late plays, has done much to dispel that fog — itself a legacy, in part, of Stanislavsky — for British theatre-goers, and these early comedies form a fitting and triumphant conclusion to his work. In a short prologue, Frayn draws attention to Chekhov's ambiguous feelings about the theatre. He hated 'theatricality', and much of the humour of these pieces lies in exposing the way people cloak themselves in affectation ('emotional fancy-dress', as Lillian Hellman has described it) in order to lend their actions some spurious drama.

Adam Lively, *'Times Literary Supplement*, 7 Oct. 1988, p. 1113

Frayn's idea to create an evening of Chekhovian fun from these short plays and some of the stories was an excellent one: it puts Chekhov into the right context. The resulting evening — a cabaret or revue-type sequence of eight separate pieces, fluently and informally linked, is delightful entertainment. . . . Frayn's text has his usual elegance and idiomatic ease.

Martin Esslin, Plays International, Nov. 1988, p. 18-19

Frayn on Chekhov

It's true that he has become very popular. I don't really know why. I suppose one of the bad reasons is that he's thought to be writing affectionately about a vanished age of leisure, and people feel a nostalgic interest in that world. Actually he's not writing with affection, and he's not writing about a world of leisure. He's writing very harshly about a world that's mostly composed of work. . . . I don't think Chekhov is at all the warm lovable writer he's sometimes held to be. I think he's absolutely dispassionate about people. He's on their side in the sense that he has a tremendous sense of their reality, but at the same time he does stand outside when we see them in all their pettiness, in all their futility. . . .

To translate a play well, you've got to understand it as a play. You've got to see what the dynamics of the play are, where the scenes hinge, which direction a scene is going in, how apparently otherwise unimportant lines are in fact advancing the plot of the play.

Frayn, interviewed by Mick Martin, 'A Not So Cosy Bear',
Plays International, Sept. 1988, p. 18-19

One of the things I've discovered in translating Chekhov's plays is how strongly plotted they are. I think that's something which is not always noticed. The whole point of his last four plays is to work against the traditional sense of the plot, and to try to catch that sense of life where things just seem to happen. Even when strong events do happen, they don't have the effect that we thought they would have. Since that's the point of those last four plays, people often don't seem to realize how beautifully organized they are. The characters just seem to say what they feel, but in fact those plays are very tightly plotted and this is why they hold our attention. Every word of those last four plays is actually driving the play forward. I don't mean to make any claims for myself, but it's certainly a lesson I try to apply in my own plays: that tautness. . . . Chekhov's other play, *Ivanov*, I am baffled by. I've read the play, and read it, and reread it, and I cannot see the force of that play. I've been asked several times to translate it, and it's just been done in London. It's been produced before and a lot of people think it's a fine play, but I just can't see it. And if you can't see it, you can't translate it.

Frayn, interviewed by John L. DiGaetani,
A Search for a Postmodern Theater, p. 75-6

Any translator of Chekhov must be painfully aware of the very large number of other versions of these plays which have been made over the years, and also of Chekhov's own hostility to the whole idea of being translated — 'I can't stop them, can I? So let them translate away; no sense will come of it in any case.' All the earlier English versions, so far as I know, have been made either by people who could read the original but who had no experience in writing plays, or by English dramatists who knew the original only through the literal version of a collaborator, or through the published editions, combined often with a mysterious inner certainty about what Chekhov was saying, or what he ought to have been saying if only he had been more like themselves. My only qualification for trying again is that I happen both to know Russian and to write plays. Translating a play is rather like writing one. The first principle, surely, is that each line should be what that particular character would have said at that particular moment if he had been a native English-speaker. This involves inhabiting that character, or trying to, as intimately as if he were one's own. The second basic principle, it seems to me, is that every line must be as immediately comprehensible as it was in the original; there are no footnotes in the theatre, and no turning back to a previous page. Practical difficulties arise in applying these principles, particularly with familiar references to matters that are unfamiliar to a modern English audience. I have expanded some of these, and cut others. . . . The other general problem is that of names. . . . These characters must all become native English-speakers, and native English-speakers do not attempt foreign words and names. I have therefore simplified ruthlessly.

Frayn, 'A Note on the Translation',
Chekhov, *Plays* (1988), p. 352-4

Frayn on Translation

[Translation] is a very good way of coming into contact with these great plays. You have to read them several times, have a perception of the characters, and understand the plot very clearly, which is harder than it might seem. They are very complex plots. All that very casual conversation advancing the plot. Obviously, the actors and the director have to get it clear in rehearsal but, if you haven't sorted it out, there is no way they will. . . . I read the text in Russian many, many times, and read around it — letters and diaries in particular. . . . You can't just find replacements line by line, word by word, you've got to get into the minds of the characters. How people come upon the words they do is philosophically and psychologically very opaque but, as a translator, you somehow have to penetrate it.

Frayn, interviewed by Mark Lawson,
'The Mark of Frayn', *Drama*, No. 3 (1988), p. 8

The question of anachronism is a difficult one. I agree one can't write a nineteenth-century play into nineteenth-century English but it seems to me that one does have to avoid glaring anachronism. . . .

The whole process of translating seems to me very much like actually writing the original play. I mean, you've somehow got to put yourself back in the position the writer was in, where the thing was in his head, before he'd actually got it down on the paper. And you've got to get those characters speaking in English instead of the original language. It feels rather like writing your own stuff. . . . I must say I find it an absolutely beguiling process. . . . In any author who's worth translating, there are a lot of difficult things, things which you wouldn't expect the characters to say – things that are awkwardly rooted in the original thinking. If you simply ignore those, if you say, well, it would be easier to say this, and to forget that, all the flavour of the original goes. And I think that's what often happens with things that are done in adaptation, or by scissors and paste methods. You do actually lose the texture of the original. There is a genuine problem: there simply aren't enough people who can write plays, and who can speak all the world's languages in which plays are written. . . . I've been very struck by seeing one or two of my own plays in other countries, where the setting has been shifted to that country, and the characters have become citizens of that country. Often it works very well and it's very intriguing to see the framework of the play shifted into a different texture, a different culture altogether. . . . It is curious that translations do seem to have a shorter shelf life than the originals. If you go back and look at the old translations of Chekhov, they do look very peculiar now, and they don't seem like Chekhov. Whereas the original Chekhov seems to me not to have dated, still to be fresh and alive and not seem old fashioned in any way.

Frayn, in discussion, Oct. 1989, printed in Translation,
National Theatre Platform Papers, No. 1 (1992)

c: Television Plays

Jamie on a Flying Visit

Transmitted: 'Wednesday Play', BBC-1, 17 Jan. 1968 (dir. Claude Whatham; with Anton Rodgers as Jamie and Dinsdale Landen as Ian).
Published: with *Birthday* (Methuen, 1990).

The rich, amiable, egocentric Jamie and his girl friend drop in on his old Oxford girl friend, Lois, whom he has not seen for seven years. She is married to a teacher and has three small children; they live in a small, untidy house. Jamie's 'flying visit' turns into staying for dinner and then for the night. His clumsy ways lead to spillings and breakages. Next day, helping to carry a divan downstairs, he treads on a toy, breaking his leg and smashing the bannisters. Soon, leg in plaster, he is comfortably settled in. Attempting to drive, he damages two cars. He invites all his friends over and at the end they take him off to dinner, ignoring Lois.

The play made clever use of the devices of the French farce in a tight little English setting. This made the humorous contrast between the mildly melancholic characters in their totally ridiculous situations all the more effective.

Stanley Reynolds, The Guardian, 18 Jan. 1968

Birthday

Transmitted: 'Wednesday Play', BBC-1, 12 Feb. 1969 (dir. Claude
  Whatham; with Angela Pleasence as Liz, Georgina Ward as Willa,
  Rosemary Leach as Jess, and Clive Swift as Neil).
Published: with *Jamie on a Flying Visit* (Methuen, 1990).

Liz's twenty-seventh birthday, on a summer Sunday in a West London flat. Her very pregnant elder sister, Jess, comes for lunch. Also present are Willa, her social worker flatmate, with her taciturn boyfriend, and the uninvited Neil, shy, pill-popping, and pursuing Liz. After an outing to a coffee bar and cinema, Jess goes into labour and insists on having the baby in the flat, encouraged by Willa (who knows all about Lamaze breathing techniques), forcing Liz and Neil together.

Beyond a Joke

Sketches for series featuring Eleanor Bron, BBC-2, Apr.-May 1972.
Published: eight sketches ('Listen to This', 'Confession', 'Blots', 'Value
  for Money', 'Who Do You Think You Are?', 'Glycerine', 'Heaven',
  and 'The Messenger's Assistant') in *Listen to This* (Methuen, 1990).

The first *Beyond a Joke* was feeling for a touch and pretty drear; the second was terrific; the third, patchy. . . . By the time Barrie Ingram got revving with his sex-appeal Eleanor Bron started to light up, and John Bird is on his best form since that long stretch in the satire mill burned his inspiration to a frazzle. With Frayn's writing as an extra ingredient, this series should be at least as good as *Where Was Spring?* A necessary tradition, this, occupying the sane and sophisticated middle attitudes.

Clive James, *The Listener*, 11 May 1972, p. 631

Making Faces

Six-part series featuring Eleanor Bron, BBC-2, 25 Sept.-30 Oct. 1975. *Unpublished.*

Begins with Zoya teaching English to foreign students in 1970, turns to her Cambridge undergraduate days ten years earlier, shows her relationships with a Tory MP, a diplomat, a married man with five children, and a bank robber, with her trying to assess her life in the last episode.

It's high-class sit-com. The BBC couldn't decide whether it was light entertainment or drama. Perhaps they should have a Department of Heavy Entertainment.

Frayn, interviewed by Ian Jack, 'Frayn, Philosopher of the Suburbs', *Sunday Times*, 13 Apr. 1975, p. 43

'I did not succeed to watch the television', explained the French student in the first episode of Michael Frayn's *Making Faces*. 'The last weekend I did not succeed to do nothing.' 'Anything', said his English language teacher, Eleanor Bron. 'No', he insisted. 'Anything is *not* what I did not. *Nothing* is what I did not.' Such elementary confusion at the language barrier amounts to a holiday for Frayn's characters, whose most anxiety-ridden dealings with English grammar and syntax take place within their own consciousness: it is in talking to themselves that they teeter at the cliff of unmeaning. 'It's not the effect that you have on me', Bron explains to her boy-friend, who might as well not be there, 'it's the effect that I have on you. Or rather, it's the effect that the effect I have on you has on me.' (I think I noted that down correctly.) Frayn is deeply and continuously concerned with Wittgenstein's philosophy, especially in its later phases, when the subject became language games, leading to brain-boggling speculations about the prospect of a game without rules. . . . Frayn has the mature humourist's horror of gags to no purpose. . . . The desire is to carry the comic vision through to its consequences.

Clive James, *The Observer*, 5 Oct. 1975, p. 22

Set in 1970, it featured Miss Bron teaching English to a succession of foreign persons by throwing her life at them (in the first half) and silently listening to their anecdotes (in the second). Dividing the play was Miss Bron's search for herself in a hotel in Nuneaton. Dulcie Gray as the hotel's owner was splendid in her solicitude, and Miss Bron made wonderful faces at herself in the mirror, in between asking, with increasing despair: 'Who *am* I?' Answer found she none, which is, I suppose, what depressed her into silence for most of what followed. The definition that finally came to her was, I think, 'the empty space at the centre of the universe', but far from that driving her over the brink, she found someone who actually shared her delusion — I mean definition — and that was the end of that. A lot of words, a lot of carefully-timed fades to avoid absolute collapse into inconsequence: I hope this series will prove more than a series of good lines written around grimaces.

Peter Buckman, *The Listener*, 2 Oct. 1975, p. 446

First and Last

Transmitted: BBC-1, 12 Dec. 1989 (dir. Alan Dossor; with Joss Ackland as Alan, Pat Heywood as Audrey, Lionel Jeffries as Laurence, and Patricia Routledge as Ivy).
Published: Methuen, 1989.

Alan, 65 years old, shy and quiet, with health problems, sets out on his lifetime's ambition to walk from Land's End to John O'Groats. Along the way he meets such people as assorted bed-and-breakfast landladies, a tramp, a girl quarrelling with her boyfriend, and a friendly hill-farmer's wife in Yorkshire. We also see frequently his puzzled wife in suburban London, and his two married children and their families, with glimpses of their lives, such as a growing friendship between sister and sister-in-law. Across the street are the friendly neighbours, Laurence and Ivy. Laurence never leaves the house and, when he tries, finds himself in hospital. The family display varied and changing attitudes to Alan's adventure — irritation, scepticism, admiration. Throughout we are unsure whether or not Alan will reach his goal, despite his ill health.

The strength of the writing lay in the wickedly observant comic treatment of the reactions of the various close relatives he leaves behind, either exclaiming about his wilful stupidity, worrying about his health, or preparing celebratory tea parties. His relationship with his wife, splendidly played by Patricia Heywood, was both understated and very moving. There was little enough, however, in the way of insights into the state of the nation as Ackland tramped the length of Britain. At considerably over two hours, the film was too long. Despite the sharp characterization, its vision of life might best be described as optimistic verging on cosy.

Malcolm Hay, 'Sight and Sound',
Plays and Players, Feb. 1990, p. 46

First and Last has a Chekhovian ring. On one level it is very funny in its acute depiction of the banalities and absurdities of ordinary life. But there is a deeper seriousness, composed of sadness and melancholy and underlined by the use of Elgar's music.

Peter Waymark, *The Times*, 12 Dec. 1989, p. 23

d: Film

Clockwise

Released: 1986 (dir. Christopher Morahan; with John Cleese as Stimpson).
Published: Methuen, 1986.

Bunyan's Pilgrim's Hymn is sung twice in Clockwise, seriously at the beginning, with heavy irony at the end. Very appropriate it is too. Firstly, because this subtle moral farce . . . is a pilgrim's progress in the form of an Ealingesque road-movie. Secondly, because the hymn provides the essential link between two gatherings and two men. The initial gathering is the morning assembly at a Midlands comprehensive school, run like a cross between Arnold's Rugby and Stalag Luft III by the dedicated Brian Stimpson (John Cleese), a time-obsessed headmaster punctilious to a fault (or Fawlty). Later that day he is to attend the annual meeting at Norwich of the Headmasters' Conference as its first chairman from a comprehensive, and it is at this august assembly the hymn is sung again.

The two men are Stimpson and his feckless music-master Mr. Jolly (Stephen Moore), who is called upon to provide the piano accompaniment on both occasions. The successful, over-organized Stimpson and the chaotic, dreaming failure Jolly are polar opposites who recur throughout Frayn's plays (as in those of his mentor Chekhov), and both attract his compassion and satirical arrows. As always, Stimpson's day is planned second by second, and as he trumpets his superiority over lesser mortals we instinctively dislike him and positively will his downfall. This begins when a pompous altercation with a ticket collector results in his boarding the train on the right-hand platform only to discover too late that the Norwich train was on the left. Leaving the text of his historic speech behind him, Stimpson begins a spiralling descent towards his destination, during which he changes vehicles and clothes, becoming variously a thief, a liar, a con-man, a vandal, and a monk. . . .

Along the way, however, our view of Stimpson changes. We discover that he is by nature a hopeless timekeeper, incapable of distinguishing left from right, who has imposed a cruelly distorting steel discipline upon himself. . . . Stimpson is brought down from within, his moral armour eroded by the panic of his soul. This tragi-comic hero's hubris is the betrayal of his pupils, his class, and his profession by his snobbish aspirations to be chairman of the Headmasters' Conference. Just at the point when we begin to feel sympathetic towards Stimpson, a brilliantly funny sequence introduces us to the public-school headmasters, a collection of grey, smugly-confident figures, wholly preoccupied with money and social prestige. In wishing to shine in their company, Stimpson is not aspiring beyond his station, he is imbued with a false social ethos and the wrong educational aims. We realize that his confusion on the railway platform between left and right was a matter of political choice, not mere chance. So, rather than being embarrassed for Stimpson when he arrives at Norwich mad and dishevelled, we are exhilarated at the prospect of him affronting and disconcerting the toffee-nosed gathering.

Philip French, 'Fawlty Meets Frayn', *The Observer*, 16 Mar. 1986

I had always wanted to write something about a man who is late because I have considerable problems in relation to that myself, and only get to places early by an enormous expenditure of psychic energy. . . . The difference between writing for film and theatre is that on stage you have a small number of people saying things in a small area and there's not much more they can do. With a film, all these limitations are removed: people can do almost anything almost anywhere.

Frayn, interviewed by David Newport, 'Three of the Best',
The Guardian, 1 Aug. 1985

Laura (Sharon Maiden), like most people of her age, has long since learned to befriend disorder and has the initiative to circumvent it, provided those in authority will let her. 'It's not a *free*, Laura, it's a private study period', Stimpson insists, in one of the last moments when such distinctions seem important. . . . This is classic comedy, revealing fears and touching on truths; the fragility of authority, the difference between right and 'right?'; and, movingly, when Stimpson, still just able to imagine that there might be a reprieve from catastrophe, says: 'It's not the despair, Laura, I can stand the despair. It's the *hope*.'

Robin Buss, *Times Educational Supplement*, 20 Mar. 1986

a: Novels

The Tin Men

Published: Collins, 1965.

The novel is set in the William Morris Institute of Automation Research; its plot revolves around the financing and opening of a new wing. The collection of odd characters includes the sports fanatic who tries to be responsible for security, the would-be novelist who cannot get further than writing the blurb and reviews for his non-existent book, and the researcher who reads everything backwards 'setting himself and solving outrageous problems of comprehension in every paragraph'. Most of the fun involves computers: the automatizing of football because the director believes 'the main object of organized sports is to produce a profusion of statistics'; the programmed newspaper, which prints the core of familiar stories such as 'I Test New Car' and 'Child Told Dress Unsuitable by Teacher'; and Delphic I, the Ethical Decision Machine, which expresses the depth and intensity of its moral processes in units called pauls, calvins, and moses. The story ends: 'Epoch IV is a computer that writes books and The Tin Men *is its first novel.'*

There were far too many moments in this book when I found my smile, but not my attention, becoming fixed. The reason is simple: *The Tin Men* is repetitive. . . . Was it perhaps too easy? You'll smile all right at *The Tin Men*, but it'll be the smile you give to a good joke you've heard before, instead of the quick stab of laughter, or surprised assent, at the sharp truth mockingly presented, fresh and original.

Julian Gloag, Saturday Review, 15 Jan. 1966, p. 40

In the past he has exposed so brilliantly some of the many vulgarities of modern life — the insidious message of the advertisement, the creepy crookedness of our PR workers, the stupidities conceived daily in our boardrooms — that he has become the only hatchet man of contemporary letters to combine a consistent attack with something that looks like a purpose. In *The Tin Men*, Mr. Frayn satirizes and parodies, probes and pounces, with all his considerable skill. This is a funny book and delightful to read; but it doesn't quite work as a novel. It is more like a particularly good Frayn piece blown up to size, with extra bits added and a plot thrown in. The characters really *are* tin men – templates for thousands of others, representatives of this disorder or that.

William Trevor, *The Listener*, 21 Jan. 1965, p. 115

The Russian Interpreter

Published: Collins, 1966.

An English research student in Moscow serves as an interpreter for a mysterious businessman who seeks ordinary Russians for exchange trips: then they become involved with a Russian girl. Though the streets and weather are carefully described, the action soon moves swiftly. Books are stolen and sought, someone is tricking someone else, espionage or smuggling is occurring, and the reader continues, waiting for explanations. Even when the two Englishmen are imprisoned, the tone remains cheerful, and the story predictably ends with their releases and flight home to England.

Proctor-Gould . . . bears a striking resemblance to Greville Wynne, the British salesman who in fact ran secrets for Russian Spy Oleg Penkovsky before the Soviets nabbed them both in 1962. . . . The implication is that Proctor-Gould has sold out and is now spying for the Russians. But is he really? Frayn doesn't say. The effect is illogical but somehow appropriate, as it is, perhaps, in real-life espionage.

Time, 21 Oct. 1966

Maybe it won't be without effect on the Cold War itself that the entertainment media men have gone over in a big way to spoofing it. Michael Frayn stands rather apart, because he doesn't invent absurdities so much as respond to real ambiguities in the situation. . . . Working for one's country is hardly distinct from working against it, or public duty from private enterprise. Mr. Frayn is as clever with these moot points as a one-man Ilf and Petrov; and since their day there haven't been many other novels about Russia so nicely poised between satire and sympathy. I only wonder if it isn't a bit too gentle, a bit droll merely. He deals with comparatively minor mishaps of the Cold War that are nobody's fault. There's hardly a hint that anyone on either side could behave really badly.

Robert Taubman, *New Statesman*, 1 Apr. 1966, p. 477

It is a serious, rather mournful story about the shabby half-world of deceit that surrounds dealings, on even the most personal level, between East and West. . . . Proctor-Gould, when he materializes, is first-rate: a figure not only of fun but of a rather sinister seediness somewhere midway between Mr. Norris and Apthorpe of *Men at Arms*. . . . He writes extremely well, with occasional echoes of the cadences of Mr. Waugh; nor would his dialogue be unworthy of that master. Indeed he writes like a modern classic, for the whole form of his novel is traditional, even though the theme with which it deals is very much of our time, while its implicit judgements suggest genuine feeling rather than the usual assumed sophistication.

Times Literary Supplement, 31 Mar. 1966, p. 257

Towards the End of the Morning

Published: Collins, 1967 (in the US under the title *Against Entropy*).

The title points to the growing sense of life being circumscribed which comes in the mid-thirties (the hero 'had spent his youth as one might spend an inheritance, and he had no idea of what he had bought with it'). The 37-year-old protagonist is a features editor, gathering crosswords and the columns for 'Meditations' and 'The Country Day by Day'. Endlessly worried about repairs to his Victorian house with West Indian neighbours in SW23, he dreams of escape and believes that appearing on a television panel could make this possible. The plot is a vehicle for the comedy of a newspaper office, and the story ends farcically as the man desperately tries to catch a plane back from the Middle East in time for his television show.

What I had the sense to do in *Towards the End of the Morning* was divide myself among the three principal protagonists — parcel myself out among Dyson, Bob, and Erskine Morris, the appalling new man. That's taken the curse off it. I don't feel got at by any of the three characters because I don't entirely identify with any of them. I also like the fact that the book's not making a point or trying to sell a bill of goods. And then again it comes out of a period in my life for which I feel affection: I like newspapers and the newspaper world.

Frayn, interviewed by Craig Raine, 'The Quarto Interview',
Quarto, No. 4 (Mar. 1980), p. 6

In parts it is uncannily like home life in our dear old Printing House Square before we moved house. Nobody has ever recorded so truthfully and so funnily the facts about the nutters who besiege the front door of a newspaper with messages from God, expenses (or exes, as we call them in the trade, to make their petty accountancy sound less of a nightmare), galley proofs, and freebies or facility trips, in which commercial enterprises try to buy favourable editorial mention by flying assorted hacks somewhere to look at something. . . . Apart from the farce in the newspaper office, and its out-stations like the King's Arms and international airports, the book is also wistfully comic and perceptive about the hang-ups of middle-class, middle-aged man, not sure about where he is going, or why, or if he will like it when he gets there.

Philip Howard, *The Times*, 4 Feb. 1978

There's something of Amis's derision but without his intolerance; there's a little of Osborne's abrasive acuteness, but none of his bitterness. Frayn's baffled liberalism sees too clearly that it takes all sorts to make a problem, that clearly defined attitudes are inherently at odds with the murky, confusing contingencies which a sensitive observer ought also to note. . . . Frayn's previous novels evoked comparison with Evelyn Waugh, but actually he is nothing like so heartless, although quite as funny. The women in *Towards the End of the Morning* — the clueless Tessa, Bob's girl, and Dyson's wife — are treated with much gentleness. The Dyson marriage, in fact, comes through with remarkable solidity, considering that it is a condition of the novel, rather than its subject.

Stephen Wall, *The Observer*, 4 June 1967

In the end the theme is time, is change, is quite simply the business of people, institutions, and society growing older. There is a marvellous passage on the funeral of old Eddy Moulton, the journalist 'long past retiring age' who at the start of the book is sitting in the corner of Dyson's office compiling the 'In Days Gone By' column. Mr. Frayn is not a philosopher for nothing, and for all the lightness of his writing he has something fresh to say here about death itself and about our attitudes to it. . . . The reader somehow feels that he has been cut short in mid-novel: that a much more extensive and ambitious book, not just an ambitious theme, has been rushed to an unresolved conclusion in the farcical last chapter. . . . One wants more leisurely treatment, and where the reader's sympathies have become so engaged with the characters it is disquieting to have to abandon them all in such a mess. . . . It takes a very good writer to pose the problems so economically, so amusingly, so humanely. But Mr. Frayn is a good enough writer to do rather more.

Times Literary Supplement, 8 June 1967

A Very Private Life

Published: Collins, 1968.

Written in the future tense, the novel begins, 'Once upon a time there will be a little girl called Uncumber.' In this world, 'inside people' remain all their lives in windowless houses, making contact by 'holo-

vision' and receiving supplies by tube and tap. During their long lives they use drugs (such as Pax, Hilarin, and Orgasmin) for every experience. In chapters of two and three pages, Frayn explains how life has grown more private, first through physical privacy, then through the development of drugs to cope with anger and uncertainty. The opening pages set the scene slowly; then Uncumber, dissatisfied with her life, seeks out a man on the other side of the world, whom she has met through a wrong number on holovision. Found, he turns out to be an 'outside person', speaking a language unknown to her, living in a decaying palace by the sea, and going out daily to work. Eventually leaving him, she is lost in a jungle and spends a night with some bandits before being found by the Kind People and rehabilitated as an 'inside person'.

The elite of the novel wear only dark glasses. To remove them is to be naked and indecent. This is the ritual covering and uncovering of American women, who wear dark glasses so that their eyes and their feelings shall not be seen. The insulated houses of the novel owe something to those of middle-class America, and in particular to those farmhouses in deepest Connecticut, abandoned when the farmers went west, surrounded by forest, and now being bought by city people to be alone.

> Frayn, interviewed by Terry Coleman,
> *The Guardian*, 1 Oct. 1968, p. 6

The book's ultimate virtue is the rigorous, brilliant intelligence with which Frayn holds its stuff within a totally consistent universe. . . . Frayn handles all his observations and inventions so brilliantly, and controls his tone so excellently, that it can only add to [his] reputation.

> Malcolm Bradbury,
> *Manchester Guardian Weekly*, 10 Oct. 1968

It is an outstanding short book which nobody else could have written, and it ought to be put into the classic modern repertoire alongside *Animal Farm*. . . . It would indeed be a deeply depressing book if it were not for the skill with which the author handles his material and the sanity with which he looks at it.

> *Times Literary Supplement*,
> 3 Oct. 1968, p. 1097

Nightmares of the future have often been dominated by fear of the encroaching mass; Frayn has realized that what technology looks like making possible is a new kind of isolation. When all needs can be satisfied by impersonal agencies, a man can become an island quite happily. Science will make solipsism a practical proposition. *A Very*

Private Life is a logical projection into the future of our present increasing skill at shutting out uncomfortable realities. It is a product of the unease which accompanies our prosperity, the guilt we feel when we go in for central heating (ought the money to have gone to Oxfam?), the fear that our obsession with services and durables will attenuate our sense of social duty and the rights of others to the point of atrophy. . . . The prose is sharpest when it's critical — when it has a bantering relationship with current clichés of thought and word; it is less impressive as an instrument of narrative. Although the book is short, its ideas are only just enough to sustain it.

Stephen Wall,
The Observer, 29 Sept. 1968

Sweet Dreams

Published: Collins, 1973.

A typical, middle-class, thirtyish, leftish Londoner is killed and finds himself in a heaven where he can fly, speak any language, change his age, and retrieve long-lost possessions. He is assigned to invent the Matterhorn, returns to England and writes an official report on its condition, drops out to enjoy the simple country life, and bounces back as right-hand man to God — who is rich, brilliant, and upper-class, and says, 'To get anything done at all one has to move in tremendously mysterious ways.' Slowly we realize that the hero's heavenly evolution is markedly similar to his earthly one.

A Very Private Life and *Sweet Dreams* are not fantasies in the sense of being an escape from what is happening. They are a way of dealing with certain aspects of real life that are extremely difficult to describe.

Frayn, interviewed by Hugh Hebert,
'Letters Play', *The Guardian*, 11 Mar. 1975

Sweet Dreams is an ironic examination of the illogicality of the idea of heaven. I feel the same way about the idea of an ideal society on earth — they fall to pieces logically. You can improve society piecemeal, of course, but I think the awful thing about changing anything is how many other changes that one change must necessitate. You can't make one thing better without making other things worse. . . . *Sweet Dreams* is the best book, and the prose there is as good as I'll ever write. But I don't like what it reveals about me.

Frayn, interviewed by Craig Raine, 'The Quarto Interview',
Quarto, No. 4 (Mar. 1980), p. 6

Here we have yet another novel about the life which follows death – the modern fantasist's favourite theme? — though this one is very different in tone from all those that have been written before and since. . . . *Sweet Dreams* is probably his best book — a beautifully sustained satire on the limitations of middle-class good intentions, reasonableness, decency, selflessness, moderation, fairness, sound common sense, and all-round good-chappery. It is impeccably written, profound (and perhaps depressing) in its implications, and very, very funny.

> David Pringle, *Modern Fantasy: the Hundred Best Novels*
> (London: Grafton, 1988), p. 151-2

Amongst the wit and high spirits Michael Frayn brings to this tale, the satire on Howard and his friends is firm, even harsh: yet, for satire, it is curiously indulgent towards the reader. With Frayn, it is not so much a question — as in Amis's or Enright's work — of tempting the reader to sympathise with some egotist and then deftly exposing his self-indulgence in doing so, as of asking the reader to make his own moral judgements from his own knowledge of the world. He has to do the work himself, if he is to interpret Frayn's picture of Howard in Heaven as a blow-up of the cocooned, self-satisfied, prosperous modern do-gooder. This is the kind of satire which makes the reader feel better as he reads, not worse — and consequently, in the end, worse rather than better, suffering from mild moral flatulence.

> Derwent May,
> *The Listener*, 16 Aug. 1973, p. 224

In this century the successful Utopias have been those like Orwell's and Huxley's, which showed Utopia as several degrees worse than our present condition. We are too sophisticated, or we have suffered too much, to accept a view of the future as ingenuous as *News from Nowhere*. It is difficult, though, to know just how to take Mr. Frayn, who offers without discernible irony a travel brochure Heaven. . . . Frayn's intentions are probably more serious than his manner, which is almost too light in its butterfly flitting from subject to subject. When Howard proposes to build the New Jerusalem, or more exactly when a film with that title is to be made out of his report on the human condition, there is some lively comedy about the film industry. Later it is suggested that Utopia isn't enough. . . . The trouble with Mr. Frayn's irony is that in most of the book you can hardly see it without using a microscope.

> Julian Symons,
> *Sunday Times*, 5 Aug. 1973, p. 32

The Trick of It

Published: Viking, 1989.

The form is the letters of a young lecturer in English, RD, to a friend in Australia. He specializes in the work of a woman novelist, JL. He invites her to speak at his obscure university, then spends the night with her, though realizing he has found a new taboo, 'against intercourse with an author on your own reading list. . . . Somewhere in common or statute law there must be a distant parallel; illicit sexual relations with a reigning monarch, perhaps.' The rest of the outward story is of falling in love, marrying her, taking her off to live in the country at Windy Ways, impulsively giving up his job, the couple living in Abu Dhabi. More important than the external details, her next novel displeases him, and he suggests improvements, which are ignored. After this, she writes of his mother, without mentioning him: now she is feeding off his world. She will not read his writings. Meanwhile, he attempts a novel: 'I don't see why the great castle of fiction should remain the exclusive preserve of the privileged few. I don't see why it shouldn't be made over to the National Trust, and thrown open to the populace at large. It's a trade, writing, that anyone can learn, not a Masonic mystery. Part of my aim is to demonstrate that any bloody fool can do it.' He fails, for he has not 'the trick of it'. Finally, he values his letters (which we are reading), then discovers the recipient has lost them. Through all this we have to keep in mind that he is an unreliable narrator, about JL and himself.

The novel is not an attack on critics, though I suppose the critic does not come off too well, but then nor does the writer. In a sense the critic holds all the aces because he tells the story, he controls the events. . . . The critic is actually the one in the driver's seat, and that's a reversal of the normal situation. . . . *The Trick of It* is not really an attack at all on literary critics or teachers of literature. The novel tries to portray the paradox of critics on the one hand and writers on the other, and the novel tries to show how writers are parasites on life. That writer begins to use up that critic's life in her fiction, and both characters feel a bit uncomfortable with that.

Frayn, interviewed by John L. DiGaetani,
A Search for a Postmodern Theater, p. 73, 75

It is a preciously twisted idea and it could have worked well under the pressure of a more tense, more chilling style. But the style is bantering intellectualized badinage, and the 'plot', the inner plot mapped out by the secret movement of the narrator's mind, peters out feebly in self-indulgent pathos, amateurish parables, and vacant profundity ('My life is in the hands of God, just where religion teaches us it is'). It is a shame, for occasionally Frayn lifts himself up and demonstrates a capacity to write with acuity and wit.

Lawrence Osborne, The Spectator, 11 Nov. 1989, p. 56

The narrator, being an academic, prefers his novels to be highly self-conscious and 'ludic', well kitted out with distancing ironic frameworks. He'd be well pleased with this one, which is as ludic as they come (and a lot funnier than most books which parade their playfulness), eminently decodable, mouth-wateringly allusive, as crafty as Nabokov.

Andrew Davies, The Listener, 28 Sept. 1989, p. 33

Until the mid-way point of this book, Michael Frayn offers a mildly amusing account of the difference between public persona and fleshly human being, of the gulf between expectation and reality. Then the novel changes, and, without losing its mannerly and ironic tone, becomes a stranger and more discomforting creature. Technically Frayn's best achievement is to have maintained a continuous and plausible narrative tone through the two very different halves of the book. . . . Through banal-seeming questions, Frayn's narrator makes the reader ponder uncomfortable problems of imagination and literature. . . . *The Trick of It* is in the end a dark novel. Its conclusions on the selfish voracity of the creative writer are bleak but persuasive.

Sebastian Faulks, Literary Review, Sept. 1989, p. 18-19

I have not encountered such easy and delightful wit and wisdom in a new work of fiction in years. Admittedly, I am an ideal kind of reader, since this is among others an academic, or rather anti-academic novel, and its theme is what to some eyes seems the ideal intimacy, the marriage of the writer and the critic. As a writer and critic myself, I have to tell you what the book now tells you, that these twosomes are not what they seem. They should work well. Writers and critics have deep interests in common: books, literature, creativity. Writers write, and critics then criticize. Writers textualize, and critics detextualize. Writers construct, and critics deconstruct. But all marriages raise questions of power. Suppose critics deconstruct, and *then* writers must construct. . . . Uneasy forms of this ideal spousehood can quickly come to mind, the dangerous subtleties of literary exchange. And they have evidently come to Frayn's mind as he constructs the perfect comedy on the matter. . . . Like William Golding's *The Paper Men*, this is a book about who owns the livingness of the living writer; it is funny, moving, intricately constructed, and done with an observant wisdom. . . . The book is about what makes writing living, and it lives.

Malcolm Bradbury, Sunday Times, 24 Sept. 1989, Sec. G, p. 6

A Landing on the Sun

Published: Viking, 1991.

Jessel, a civil servant, is asked to investigate the mysterious death of Summerchild, found under a Ministry of Defence window seventeen years earlier: now a TV programme is being made about him. Jessel finds he has links with Summerchild, having gone to school with his daughter in Greenwich. Jessel finds the files (and tapes) and that Summerchild established a Policy Unit on 'the quality of life' when Harold Wilson was Prime Minister in 1974. The unit was headed by Ruth Serafin, an Oxford philosophy don, and Jessel discovers and re-creates her affair with Summerchild.

Surprisingly Frayn, whose early novels were so funny, opts instead for a tone of sustained melancholy which the events themselves never seem to justify. He has a serious point to make about the difference between philosophical and political concepts of happiness, but it fails to hit home because the philosophic content of the book seems so rarefied and irrelevant beside its scrupulously authentic political detail.

Jonathan Coe, *The Guardian*, 19 Sept. 1991, p. 26

There is something in the book's contrived clashes between bureaucrateze and philosophy that is reminiscent of the awkward overkill that afflicted Ian McEwan's *A Child in Time*. Like McEwan, Frayn is aiming, through an ironic use of a thriller plot chassis, to suggest how personal experience remains inscrutable. . . . *A Landing on the Sun* shares with last year's philosophy lecture, William Boyd's *Brazzaville Beach*, a temporally split-level plot that leads to a suicide provoked by thinking too much — for the death of Summerchild looks increasingly like suicide under the influence of Wittgenstein.

Tom Shone, *The Observer*, 13 Oct. 1991, p. 58

How much of what Jessel records of Summerchild's and Serafin's affair is actually derived from tapes and how much either from imagination or from intimations beamed in on him by the dead man's ghost, haunting the claustrophobic eyrie still full of the pathetic relics of his cohabitation with his middle-aged mistress, is never wholly clear; and that it should not be clear is part of the fascination of the story. Jessel's role is, essentially, that of any novelist. What he writes about the tragedy and comedy of human existence is derived in part from the evidence of what he sees, hears, and reads, but, in even greater part, from what he intuits and imagines. As he is haunted by Summerchild and Serafin, so every novelist is intermittently haunted by his characters. Jessel's increasing

75

self-identification with Summerchild is a paradigm of every novelist's increasing self-identification with his narrator/protagonist.

Francis King, *The Spectator*, 14 Sept. 1991, p. 31-2

Mr. Frayn's new novel . . . is again in a sense a philosophical fable inquiring into the nature of happiness, but it is also his first work to combine most of the skills from all his careers. It is a very funny satire on bureaucracies, particularly the British Civil Service, and partly a spy novel or whodunit, sewn with small Hitchcock shivers. . . . In part it turns into a play, or at least a dialogue to which the protagonist is audience. Certainly Mr. Frayn has learned from his years in the theatre how to dramatize a story through its characters, so that this fable reads like a 'real' novel more often than it lets you recognize it as a kind of parody of *The Castle* by Kafka. . . . *A Landing on the Sun* is a contrivance of an elegance and cunning reminiscent of Henry James, and Mr. Frayn's most artful creation so far.

Ronald Bryden,
New York Times Book Review, 16 Feb. 1992

Now You Know

Published: Viking, 1992.

At its heart is 61-year-old Terry, 'a combination of self-righteousness charming rascality, and self-satisfied humour'. Having worked as a Thames lighterman, actor, DJ, journalist, and school-teacher, and having also served a prison sentence, Terry now heads an organization, Open, dedicated to the cause of open government. He is persistent and adroit in ferreting out secrets, mounting demonstrations, recruiting supporters, grabbing headlines, arousing indignation. One of the workers in Terry's little pressure group is a barrister called Roy; and Roy has a girl-friend, Hilary, who is a seemingly dedicated Civil Servant at the Home Office. Open has been investigating a case involving the Home Office: a black man, Hassam, has been found dead, apparently as the result of police brutality, in the cell in which he was being held. 'Have we got the situation contained?' Hilary's worried colleagues ask each other. What they do not realize is that Hilary, partly disgusted with the cover-up and partly infatuated with Terry, is about to pass on to Open all the top-secret information at her disposal. Frayn tells his story, in the present tense, through now one and now another of the actors in his drama. . . . Frayn neatly contrasts Terry's demands for open government with the secrecy with which he is careful to shroud his own emotional life. This engaging wide boy is indignant because the Home Office refuses to tell the truth about Hassam's death; but he himself tells — and lives — a sequence of lies in his relationships with Jacqui and Hilary, each woman imagining that she is exclusively his lover. With the rest of his staff he is equally dishonest. In turn, all these people are to some extent dishonest with him and with each other.

Francis King, *The Spectator*, 29 Aug. 1992, p. 28

This lesson on the slipperiness of truth is familiar but fun: how people put two and two together and make the wrong end of a stick; how there are as many different realities as there are narrators; how snapshots taken through opening and closing doors come out as red herrings.

Phil Hogan, *The Observer*, 30 Aug. 1992, p. 50

Frayn spins it into a novel by writing it as a play. Every character gives his own version of events. Only the *dramatis personae* appear in this book, each speaking for himself as the action progresses. The novel is thus constructed from a series of time-consecutive, on-the-spot reports, as each player in turn offers us an account of the unfolding story. It becomes a play without stage directions or even direct dialogue, with player after player stepping forward onto the stage apron and taking the audience into their confidence with a personal soliloquy. We see it through their eyes: *all* their eyes. There is no independent narrator, no apparent authorial presence. . . . It is harder to leap out of the pages of a book, and novelists who affect this style are in danger of seeming clever rather than illuminating. Frayn is rescued by the fact that he is so consistently clever that it is almost enough. Almost. But I should not think any the less of him if he would do the decent thing, stand over my shoulder, and introduce me to his characters: tell me a little about them; comment, even — or *admit* to commenting. As a reader it is nice to *know somebody* in a novel, to feel a special intimacy with someone, be it the author or (which may amount to the same) the author's favourite character. In *Now You Know*, and with a good deal of Frayn's work, I have the eerie feeling that he has walked out of the room and left me alone with his characters. And I don't like it.

Matthew Parris, *The Times*, 10 Sept. 1992, Sec. III, p. 4

b: Humour

The following represent selections from the thrice-weekly column which Frayn wrote for The Guardian *from 1960 to 1962, and from his weekly column for* The Observer *from 1962 to 1968.*

The Day of the Dog (Collins, 1962).
The Book of Fub, in the USA *Never Put Off to Gomorrah* (Collins, 1963).

On the Outskirts (Collins, 1964).

At Bay in Gear Street (Collins, 1967).

The Original Michael Frayn, ed. James Fenton (Edinburgh: Salamander, 1983; Methuen, 1990). [Selects from all the above and adds nineteen *Observer* columns, 1967-68, not previously collected.]

Listen to This (Methuen, 1990). [Contains one piece from *The Book of Fub* and four from *On the Outskirts*, together with one from *The Independent*, a sketch written for Amnesty in 1979, and two previously unpublished, in addition to the play, *The Two of Us*, and eight sketches from the television series, *Beyond a Joke*.]

Frayn is equally at home writing brief lives of Harold Wilson, Mozart, and T. S. Eliot in their own styles, and contrasting the Horace and Doris Morris style of interior decor with Mies van der Rohe, and although he makes it look easy this collection shows how much this whole genre — perhaps it should be called Fraynery — owes to him. It also shows how much better his work is than the lukewarm facetiousness of his imitators. Read in one go at book length, however, Frayn is almost too clever, funny, militantly liberal, and cultured, and the effect is all a little bit Hampstead.

Sunday Times, 9 Sept. 1990, Sec. VII, p. 8

They weren't really satire at all but simple social observation. For this reason the twenty intervening years haven't dated his characters. . . . The only pieces in this book which seem locked in their period are those in which Frayn was parodying the journalism of the time, and particularly the tone of breathless upbeat silliness which marked the popular press.

Simon Hoggart, *The Observer*, 13 Nov. 1983

Frayn's future, or rather future perfect, dramatic development is foreshadowed . . . in a number of striking theatrical pieces, most notably where he exchanges the scalpel for the custard pie, . . . the method of precision for the method of cumulation, the timing of the epigrammatist for that of the *farceur*.

Eric Korn, *Times Literary Supplement*, 3 Feb. 1984, p. 118

c: Philosophy

Constructions

Published: Wildwood House, 1974.

These 309 numbered homilies, reveries, and speculations make nods of acknowledgement to Wittgenstein and Pascal, but they are actually the secret marginalia of a novelist who understands how the world works because he has created worlds too.

> Jonathan Raban, 'Is God a Novelist?', *Sunday Times*, 3 Nov. 1974

Constructions is a fascinating and endlessly thought-provoking little book of a kind which is so difficult to categorize that it might almost be described as unique. It is poetical; it is philosophical (yet anti-philosophizing!); and it is a genuine contribution to psychology. . . . This is not only an unusually cheerful book: it is also a witty one.

> Philip Toynbee, *The Observer*, 20 Oct. 1974

It is a philosophical treatise, a wrestle with a set of identifiably philosophical problems, and sometimes the method of sober, prose argument is used in it. More often, though, it works with aphorisms, jokes, metaphors, analogies, questions: the final effect of the work is enlightenment, which is comparable with what linear argument can produce; but the means of its production are more like poetry than prose and there is also something special about what is produced. For example, when Mr. Frayn remarks that 'A man dominates his environment by establishing a unifying principle — himself', and compares this with 'a tank laying its own tracks across the wilderness', something is achieved, for me anyway, which lies outside the reach of the more prosaic means of academic philosophy. . . . I am glad that he did what he did, namely to write what may be the only unboring and unembarrassing attempt, other than Wittgenstein's own, to do philosophy in a manner which deliberately eschews theory and proceeds by something like the assembling of reminders for a purpose.

> Jonathan Bennett, *Times Literary Supplement*, 20 June 1975, p. 693

d: Journalism

'Festival', *The Age of Austerity, 1945-51*, ed. Michael Sissons and Philip French (Hodder and Stoughton, 1963), p. 330-52. [On the Festival of Britain, 1951. Shrewdly divides Britons into Herbivores, 'the radical middle-classes — the do-gooders; the readers of the *News Chronicle*, the *Guardian* and the *Observer*; the signers of petitions; the backbone of the BBC . . . guiltily conscious of their advantages', and the Carnivores, 'the readers of the *Daily Express*; the Evelyn Waughs; the cast of the *Directory of Directors*', a 'split in the privileged classes'. Herbivores dominated in the 1940s.]

'On the Riviera', *The Observer*, 22 Aug. 1965.

'Russell and Wittgenstein', *Commentary* (New York), May 1967, p. 68-75.

'Return to Paradise', *The Observer*, 4 June 1967.

'Writers on Trial: Thoughts on the Sinyavsky-Daniel Case', *Encounter*, Jan. 1968, p. 80-8.

'Frayn in Cuba', *The Observer*, 12 Jan., 19 Jan., 26 Jan. 1969.

'The Last Time I Saw Paris', *The Observer*, 25 May 1969.

'Reassessment: a Battle Against Bewitchment', *New Statesman*, 22 Aug. 1969. [On Wittgenstein.]

'Little Israel', *The Observer*, 14 Sept. 1969.

'Greater Israel', *The Observer*, 21 Sept. 1969.

'Made in Manchester', *The Observer*, 2 May 1971. [On the 150th anniversary of the *Manchester Guardian*.]

'Inner Voice', *New Statesman*, 12 May 1972. [Review of *In the Village*, by Anthony Bailey.]

'The Capital of Nowhere', *The Observer*, 6 Aug. 1972. [First of two-part series on West and East Berlin.]

'The Gnomes of Köpenick', *The Observer*, 13 Aug. 1972.

'Frayn's Japan', *The Observer*, 12 Aug., 19 Aug. 1973.

'Frayn's Sweden', *The Observer*, 21 Apr. 1974.

'A Yearning for Summer', *The Observer*, 28 Apr. 1974. [Continues foregoing report on Sweden.]

'Living in the Past', *The Observer*, 24 Aug. 1975. [On Vienna.]

'The End of the Dance', *The Observer*, 7 Sept. 1975 [On Anthony Powell's *Dance to the Music of Time*.]

'Australia: the Long Straight', *Great Railway Journeys of the World* (BBC, 1981), p. 71-95.

'Like a Breath of Fresh Air', *The Observer*, 1 Nov. 1981. [Review of *Guardian Years*, by Alastair Hetherington.]

'The Conjuring Trick of the Kurfürstendamm', *The Observer Magazine*, 11 July 1982.

'Introduction', Alan Bennett, Peter Cook, Jonathan Miller, and Dudley Moore, *The Complete Beyond the Fringe* (Methuen, 1987), p. 7-9; revised from 'Introduction' to previous edition (Souvenir Press, 1963).

'Roofless Chancels', *The Observer*, 15 May 1988. [Review of *Games with Shadows*, by Neal Ascherson.]

'Home Thoughts', *Independent Magazine*, 16 Sept. 1989.

'Michael Frayn', *Fleet Street Remembered*, ed. Tony Gray (Heinemann, 1990), p. 166-9.

'Everyday Portents of Catastrophe', *Independent on Sunday*, 16 Feb. 1990. [About Trifonov.]

'Michael Glenny', *The Times*, 3 Aug. 1990, p. 12. [Unsigned obituary.]

'The Root of All Delay', *The Spectator*, 1 Feb. 1992.

'Remembering Michael Powell', *Sight and Sound*, Oct. 1992, p. 24.

It's one of the *attractions* of writing for theatre, if you've written novels, that it does circumscribe one. As you know, what you need in any art is some kind of limitation within which to work. . . . The difficulty of writing novels, it seems to me, is that you can do absolutely anything. The novel form is open: there's almost nothing you can't do. It must, I suppose, end up as words on paper, but that's all. On the stage you're restricted to words being said by people, so you can't stop for description or for accounts of ideas. Really you can't give much account of what's going on in people's heads. . . . I think I stopped writing novels because I found it increasingly difficult to locate my own voice. One of the pleasures of writing for the stage is that it's other people's voices. . . .

What people often don't understand is that writing for the theatre is a collaborative thing. People ask one sympathetically if one is allowed any control or just brutally manhandled. It's not like that. If it is working at all, everyone (actors, director, designer) have to contribute creatively. The text is an important element but it is only one element. As a writer in rehearsals, one often feels that the thing isn't being done right, but equally often one is amazed to see actors doing things with the text that one just hadn't quite grasped oneself. Suddenly new life is breathed in by someone else where before there was no life or only half life.

Frayn, interviewed by Craig Raine, 'The Quarto Interview', *Quarto*, No. 4 (Mar. 1980), p. 4, 6

I'm still amazed by conjuring tricks. . . . I'm thinking of those heart-stopping moments when the world is transformed in front of your eyes. Sometimes by sheer surprise, as in the first scene of *The Philanthropist*, when the undergraduate exercises the stage-effect he has just described in his essay; Christopher Hampton tells you in advance exactly what the trick is going to be and how it's going to be done, and you still sit unable to breathe for five minutes afterwards. Sometimes the transformation is emotional — as when Oxenby suddenly surrenders to the moment in *The Dresser*, and leaps for the thunder-sheet he has earlier refused to touch. Sometimes the whole earth shifts, as when Joe Egg, the uninhabited shell of a living child in Peter Nichols's play, gets out of her wheelchair at the end of Act I, and runs forward playing a skipping game, so that all the bitter wrongs of the world are for one moment of hallucination righted. . . .

I sometimes feel that the skill of audiences is not always sufficiently noted. Some theatregoers arrive late, certainly, some of them comment on the performance aloud and wait for the laugh-lines to cough. But the surprising thing really is how *few* behave like this, and how many understand the conventions and are prepared to abide by them. To find two, or five, or ten good actors to perform a play is difficult; to find two hundred, or five hundred, or a thousand good people to watch it, night after night, is a miracle. . . . To be a member of a good audience is exhilarating. . . .

So far as I can see, all of these plays are attempts to show something about the world, not to change it or to promote any particular idea of it. That's not to say there are no ideas in them. In fact what they are all about in one way or another (it seems to me) is the way in which we impose our ideas upon the world around us. In *Alphabetical Order* it is by classification, in *Make and Break* by consumption. . . .

It is more fashionable these days for a writer to be chosen by his material, like an old-fashioned bride; it makes the material sound stronger and more imperious. The truth is that I don't know whether I chose it or not. Some of these characters walked into my head uninvited, and told me their story as soon as they sat down. . . . Others I dragged in off the street by force. They didn't want to talk. I had to pretend to them that I knew the whole story anyway, confront them with the confessions of their accomplices. Some of them I was forced to take down to the soundproof interrogation room and show the bloodstains on the walls. Was I uncovering the evidence, or was I creating it? Was the world telling me what it was like, or was I telling the world? The question is impossible to answer, even in theory — because of course it is just one form of the very dilemma that I am writing about.

Frayn, 'Introduction', *Plays: One*, p. xi-xiv

a: Primary Sources

Collections of Plays

*For publication of plays in individual volumes, Look Look,
the translations, television plays, and film script, see under
their respective titles in Section 2. The eight novels, five
volumes of humour, and* Constructions *are also listed in
Section 2, the miscellaneous journalism in Section 3.*

Plays: One (Methuen, 1985). [Includes *Alphabetical Order*,
    Donkeys' Years, *Clouds*, *Make and Break*, and *Noises Off*.]
Plays: Two (Methuen, 1991). [Includes *Benefactors*,
    Balmoral, and *Wild Honey*.]
Listen to This (Methuen, 1990). [Includes *The Two of Us* and
    seventeen very short pieces.]

Interviews

John Grigg, 'More than a Satirist', *The Observer*, 11 June
    1967.
Terry Coleman, 'Towards the End of Frayn's Morning', *The
    Guardian*, 1 Oct. 1968, p. 6.
Hugh Hebert, 'Letters Play', *The Guardian*, 11 Mar. 1975, p. 12.
Ian Jack, 'Frayn, Philosopher of the Suburbs', *Sunday Times*,
    13 Apr. 1975, p. 43.
Russell Davies, 'Michael Frayn, Witty and Wise', *The
    Observer*, 18 July 1976, p. 8.
Ray Connolly, 'Playwrights on Parade', *Sunday Times*, 27 Jan.
    1980, p. 32.
Craig Raine, 'The Quarto Interview', *Quarto*, No. 4
    (Mar. 1980), p. 3-6.
'Pendennis', 'Tom Frayn's Son', *The Observer*, 27 Apr. 1980,
    p. 44.
'Why Frayn Went to Mock and Stayed to Pray', *The
    Guardian*, 6 Feb. 1982.
'Mandrake', 'Frayn Refrains from the Farce', *Sunday
    Telegraph*, 11 Mar. 1984.
Benedict Nightingale, 'Michael Frayn: the Entertaining
    Intellect', *New York Times Magazine*, 8 Dec. 1985, p. 66-8,
    125-8, 133.
David Kaufman, 'The Frayn Refrain', *Horizon*, Jan.-Feb.
    1986, p. 33-6.

William A. Henry III, 'Tugging at the Old School Ties', *Time*, 27 Jan.
    1986, p. 67.
Lesley Thornton, 'Funny You Should Say That . . .', *Observer
    Magazine*, 23 Feb. 1986, p. 24-6. [On *Clockwise*, with John Cleese.]
Miriam Gross, 'A Playwright of Many Parts', *Sunday Telegraph*,
    30 Nov. 1986, p. 17.
Mark Lawson, 'The Mark of Frayn', *Drama*, No. 3 (1988), p. 7-9.
Mick Martin, 'A Not So Cosy Bear', *Plays International*, Sept. 1988, p. 18.
Mark Lawson, 'The Man Who Isn't Ayckbourn', *The Independent
    Magazine*, 17 Sept. 1988, p. 40-2.
Blake Morrison, 'Front Legs and Back Legs', *The Observer*, 17 Sept. 1989.
Penny Perrick, 'The Adaptability of Michael Frayn', *Sunday Times*,
    17 Sept. 1989, Sec. G, p. 8-9.
Heather Neill, 'Bleak Comedy of a Changing World', *The Times*,
    24 Oct. 1989, p. 15.
Stephen Pile, 'The Other Mr. Frayn', *Daily Telegraph Magazine*,
    31 Mar. 1990, p. 17-21.
Heather Neill, 'A Philosopher Speaks', *The Times*, 17 Apr. 1990.
John L. DiGaetani, *A Search for a Postmodern Theater* (New York:
    Greenwood, 1991), p. 73-81.

b: Secondary Sources

Mark Fritz, 'Michael Frayn', *Dictionary of Literary Biography, 13:
    British Dramatists since World War II*, ed. Stanley Weintraub
    (Detroit: Bruccoli Clark/Gale, 1982), p. 171-8.
John Russell Taylor, 'Only When They Laugh?', *Plays and Players*,
    Mar. 1982, p. 15-16.
Malcolm Page, 'Michael Frayn', *Dictionary of Literary Biography, 14:
    British Novelists Since 1960*, ed. Jay L. Halio (Detroit: Bruccoli
    Clark/Gale, 1983), p. 336-41.
Katharine Worth, 'Farce and Michael Frayn', *Modern Drama*, XXVI
    (Mar. 1983), p. 47-53.
Peter Roberts, 'Director as Editor?', *Plays*, Apr. 1984, p. 12-4.
    [Interview with Michael Blakemore on directing Frayn's plays.]
John Frayn Turner, 'Desperately Funny', *Plays and Players*, Dec. 1984,
    p. 8-10.
Paul Allen, 'When Truth Dazzles: the Work of Michael Frayn', *Country
    Life*, 23 May 1985, p. 1422-3.
Albert-Reiner Glaap, 'Order and Disorder on Stage and in Life: Farce
    Majeure in Frayn's Plays', *Studien zur Asthetik des Gegenswarts-
    theaters*, ed. Christian W. Thomsen (Heidelberg: Carl Winter, 1985),
    p. 195-208.

Richard Allen Cave, *New British Drama in Performance on the London Stage, 1970-1985* (Gerrards Cross: Colin Smythe, 1987), p. 61-6, 103-4.

Garry O'Connor, 'Michael Frayn', *Contemporary Dramatists*, fourth edition, ed. D. L. Kirkpatrick (St. James Press, 1988), p. 167-8.

Susan Rusinko, *British Drama, 1950 to the Present: a Critical History* (Boston: G. K. Hall/Twayne, 1989), p. 180-4.

Robert Hewison, 'Translating Culture into Comedy', *Sunday Times*, 25 Mar. 1990, Sec. E, p. 6.

Hugh Hebert, 'Last Laugh of a Truth Stranger than Farce', *The Guardian*, 16 Apr. 1990, p. 9.

Anon., 'Michael Frayn', *The Observer Book of Profiles*, ed. Robert Low (W. H. Allen, 1991), p. 170-3. [Reprinted from *The Observer*, 1 Apr. 1984.]

Vera Gottlieb, 'Why this Farce?', *New Theatre Quarterly*, No. 27 (Aug. 1991), p. 217-28. [On Frayn and Chekhov.]

Christopher Innes, *Modern British Drama 1890-1990* (Cambridge University Press, 1992), p. 312-24.